SCOTT FORESMAN

Art

Robyn Montana Turner, Ph.D.
Program Author

Editorial Offices: Glenview, Illinois • Parsippany, New Jersey • New York, New York

Sales Offices: Parsippany, New Jersey • Duluth, Georgia • Glenview, Illinois • Coppell, Texas • Ontario, California • Mesa, Arizona

Program Consultants

Christopher Adejumo, Ph.D.
Associate Professor
Visual Art Studies
University of Texas
Austin, Texas

Doug Blandy, Ph.D.
Professor and Director
Arts and Administration Program
Institute for Community Arts and Studies
University of Oregon
Eugene, Oregon

Rebecca Brooks, Ph.D.
Professor
Department of Art and Art History
University of Texas
Austin, Texas

Sara A. Chapman, Ed.D.
Director of Fine Arts
Alief Independent School District
Houston, Texas

James Clarke, M.Ed.
Executive Director
Texas Coalition for Quality Arts Education
Houston, Texas

Georgia Collins, Ph.D.
Professor Emeritus
College of Fine Arts
University of Kentucky
Lexington, Kentucky

Deborah Cooper, M.Ed.
Coordinating Director of Arts Education
Curriculum and Instruction
Charlotte-Mecklenburg Schools
Charlotte, North Carolina

Sandra M. Epps, Ph.D.
Multicultural Art Education Consultant
New York, New York

Mary Jo Gardere
Multi-Arts Specialist
Eladio Martinez Learning Center
Dallas, Texas

Carlos G. Gómez, M.F.A.
Professor of Fine Art
University of Texas at Brownsville
and Texas Southmost College
Brownsville, Texas

Kristina Lamour, M.F.A.
Assistant Professor
The Art Institute of Boston
at Lesley University
Boston, Massachusetts

Melinda M. Mayer, Ph.D.
Assistant Professor
School of Visual Arts
University of North Texas
Denton, Texas

Reviewers

Studio Reviewers

Judy Abbott, *Art Educator*
Allison Elementary School
Austin Independent School
District
Austin, Texas

Lin Altman, *Art Educator*
Cedar Creek Elementary
School
Eanes Independent School
District
Austin, Texas

Geral T. Butler, *Art Educator*
(Retired)
Heritage High School
Lynchburg City Schools
Lynchburg, Virginia

Dale Case, *Elementary Principal*
Fox Meadow Elementary
School
Nettleton School District
Jonesboro, Arkansas

Deborah McLouth, *Art Educator*
Zavala Elementary School
Austin Independent School
District
Austin, Texas

Patricia Newman, *Art Educator*
Saint Francis Xavier School
Archdiocese of Chicago
La Grange, Illinois

Nancy Sass, *Art Educator*
Cambridge Elementary
School
Alamo Heights Independent
School District
San Antonio, Texas

Sue Spiva Telle, *Art Educator*
Woodridge Elementary
School
Alamo Heights Independent
School District
San Antonio, Texas

Cari Washburn, *Art Educator*
Great Oaks Elementary
School
Round Rock Independent
School District
Round Rock, Texas

Critic Readers

Celeste Anderson
Roosevelt Elementary School
Nampa, Idaho

Mary Jo Burkwocz
Wilson Elementary School
Janesville, Wisconsin

Mary Jane Cahalan
Mitzi Bond Elementary
School
El Paso, Texas

Cindy Collar
Cloverleaf Elementary School
Cartersville, Georgia

Yvonne Days
St. Louis Public Schools
St. Louis, Missouri

Shirley Dickey
Creative Art Magnet School
Houston, Texas

Ray Durkee
Charlotte Performing Arts
Center
Punta Gorda, Florida

Sue Flores-Minick
Bryker Woods Elementary
School
Austin, Texas

Alicia Lewis
Stevens Elementary School
Houston, Texas

Denise Jennings
Fulton County Schools
Atlanta, Georgia

James Miller
Margo Elementary School
Weslaco, Texas

Marta Olson
Seattle Public Schools
Seattle, Washington

Judy Preble
Florence Avenue School
Irvington, New Jersey

Tonya Roberson
Oleson Elementary School
Houston, Texas

Andrew Southwick
Edgewood Independent
School District
San Antonio, Texas

Nita Ulaszek
Audelia Creek Elementary
School
Dallas, Texas

Tessie Varthas
Office of Creative and
Public Art
Philadelphia, Pennsylvania

Penelope Venola
Spurgeon Intermediate
School
Santa Ana, California

Elizabeth Willett
Art Specialist
Fort Worth, Texas

Contents

Unit 1

Art and You 16

Martin Ramirez.
*Untitled (Horse and
Rider),* 1954.

Unit 2

Grandma Moses.
December, 1943.

1

Unit 3

Art, Past and Present 84

Susan Stinsmuehlen.
Knight Giant, Oil and Wind, 1985.

Unit 4

Art as Self-Expression...........118

Henri Matisse.
The Thousand and One Nights, 1950.

Unit 5

All Kinds of Art 152

Romare Bearden. *Morning of the Rooster,* 1980.

Unit 6

More Ideas for Art 186

Alfred Stieglitz.
The Steerage, 1907.

Start with Art

When you write a story, you may ask the questions: *Who, What, When, Where, Why*, and *How*. Finding the answers to these questions can help you develop your story.

When you explore the world of art, asking these same questions can help you understand others' artworks and create your own.

Ask yourself these questions:
    Who makes art?
    What is art?
    Where is art made?
    Why do artists make art?
    How do artists make art?

This book explores these art questions and much more. It shows you how to look at art and how to make your own artworks.

You are an artist. You see the world as an artist. This book will help you develop your art skills and find new ways to express your ideas and thoughts. You will learn to find art in unexpected places. Look around you. What do you see?

Suzanne Valadon. *The Violin Box,* 1923. Oil on canvas. Musée d'Art Moderne de la Ville de Paris.

Artist unknown. Mayan. *Female Whistle Figure with Monkey and Child,* ca. A.D. 600-900. Earthenware with pigments. Denver Art Museum Collection.

Imagine yourself as a working artist. What skills will you need to know?

Your Art Words

To understand art, it is important to understand the language of art. Your book contains many art words. They are shown in **yellow.** These words help artists talk about art.

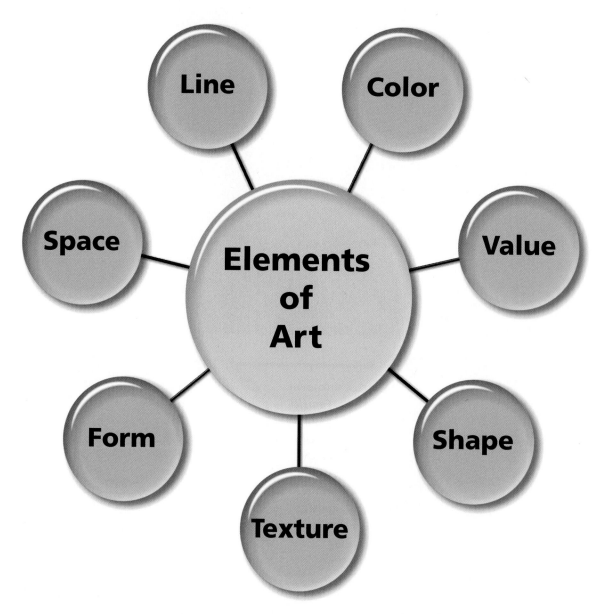

These art words name parts of an artwork.

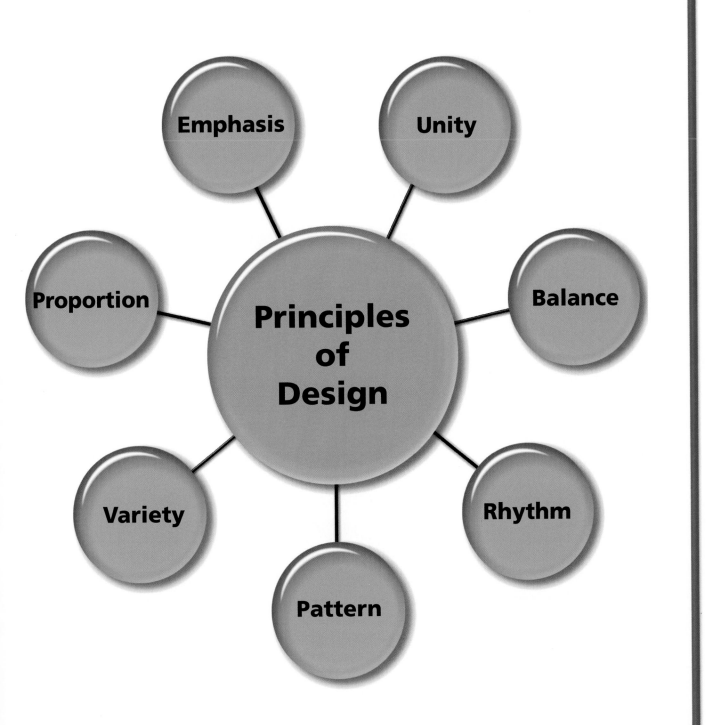

These art words tell how an artwork is put together.

Jessie T. Pettway. (Gee's Bend quilters). *Bars and String-Piece Columns,* 1950's. Cotton, 95 by 76 inches. Tinwood Alliance Collection, Atlanta, Ga.

Visit a Museum

Art museums are places that collect and display artworks. You can see artworks like this at an art museum.

Many people work in art museums. One such person is the curator. A **curator** is an art expert who collects and takes care of artworks. The curator also decides where to place the artworks.

Another person you may see at an art museum is a docent. **Docents** greet visitors and show them around the museum. They also provide information about the art and artists. They can answer questions to help you better understand the art.

What questions would you ask to form conclusions about this artwork?

Art Tools

Artists use tools to make their artworks. Different types of tools are used to create different types of art. Think about some of the art tools you would like to explore as you make your own artwork.

Chalk pastels and artists' pencils can be used for drawing.

Artists often experiment with many types of paint-brushes and other tools when painting.

These tools are used to make beautiful mosaic designs.

Ink, paint, sponges, and a roller called a brayer, are tools used in printmaking.

When artists make clay sculptures, they use some of these tools.

Photography is the art of taking pictures. The most important tools for photography are a camera and film.

12

Make a Portfolio

Artists often keep their artworks in a portfolio. You can store your flat artwork in a portfolio too. Follow these steps to make a portfolio. Use it to share your artworks with others.

1 Use two sheets of poster board. Write your name across the top of one sheet.

2 Place one sheet over the other. Be sure your name is on the front.

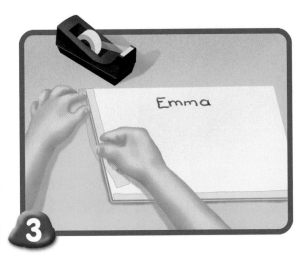

3 Tape the bottom and sides of your portfolio.

4 Use colored markers to decorate your portfolio.

Make a Sketchbook Journal

Many artists plan by drawing sketches. Sketches can help them remember what they have seen or imagined. Artists also record their thoughts and feelings with their sketches.

A sketchbook is a special tool. In it, artists can draw, paint, and even write their ideas. Later, they can use their sketches as a starting place for a larger artwork.

Look at these sketches by Frida Kahlo. How do they compare to sketches that you make?

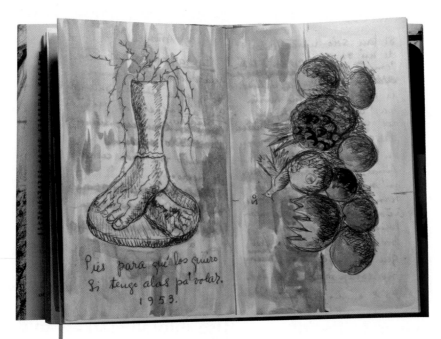

Frida Kahlo. *Sketch from the Diary of Frida Kahlo.*

Follow these steps to make a Sketchbook Journal.

1 Fold eight sheets of drawing paper in half.

2 Staple the sheets together along the fold.

3 Fold and staple a construction paper cover.

4 Decorate the cover. Write your name on it.

Georges Seurat. (Detail) *A Sunday on La Grande Jatte–1884,* 1884–1886. Oil on canvas, 83 by 123¼ inches. Helen Birch Bartlett Memorial Collection, 1926.224. Photograph © 1996, The Art Institute of Chicago.

Unit 1

Art and You

When you look at the world, use an artist's eye to appreciate what you see. Look for the **elements of art,** or line, shape, color, value, texture, form, and space, that artists use to create their artworks. Artists also use the **principles of design,** or balance, pattern, rhythm, unity, variety, emphasis, and proportion. These principles help an artist organize the elements to express ideas and feelings.

Meet the Artist

Georges Seurat spent his life studying art in Paris, France. He experimented with light and color in different ways. Instead of using lines, he used small dots of color. This technique is called Pointillism. In this unit you will see another example of Pointillism by Seurat. Look for a painting that seems to shimmer with energy and light.

Ernest Laurent. *Portrait of Georges Seurat,* 1883.

Beauty in Your World

Beauty surrounds you. You can find beauty in the **natural environment,** such as plants, rocks, and sky. You can also discover beauty in the **constructed environment.** These are the things or **objects** made by humans, such as buildings and artworks. Take a closer look at objects you see in your environments. What makes each object beautiful?

This photograph shows a natural environment. What does your natural environment look like?

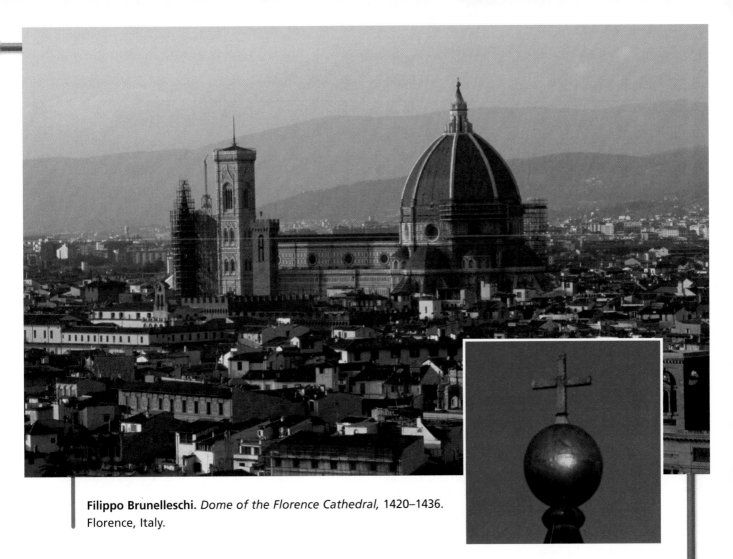

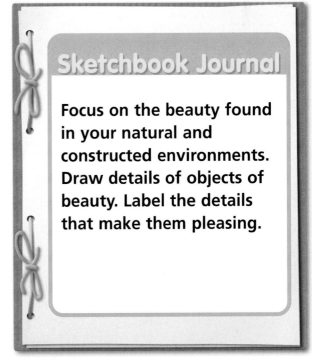

Filippo Brunelleschi. *Dome of the Florence Cathedral,* 1420–1436. Florence, Italy.

You can also discover beauty by noticing **details.** These are small parts that make up a whole. Where do you see details on these pages? Details can help you notice the elements of art in objects and artworks. They can also help you find beauty in everyday objects in your environment.

Sketchbook Journal

Focus on the beauty found in your natural and constructed environments. Draw details of objects of beauty. Label the details that make them pleasing.

Draw Ideas of Beauty

Follow the steps to draw objects from the natural and constructed environments. Decorate your drawing with objects from both environments.

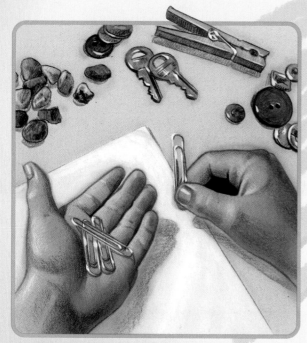

1 Collect a variety of natural and human-made objects.

2 Draw a scene that includes natural and constructed objects.

Technique Tip

Apply light pressure to the crayon when coloring so you can layer colors. Start with light colors, then add darker colors.

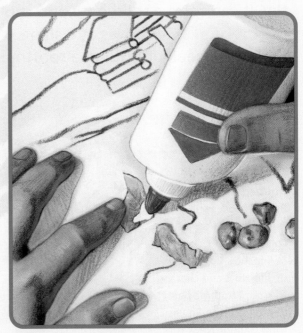

3 Choose small natural and human-made objects to decorate your drawing.

4 Glue the small objects to your drawing to add detail.

Think Like an Artist

Artists use details to make their artwork more personal, recognizable, or realistic. What kinds of details helped you add beauty to your scene?

Line

The mark a point makes as it moves across a surface is a **line.** Line is an element of art. A **vertical line** rises up like a tree or a tower and can show power and strength. A **horizontal line** matches the line that divides the earth and sky. It can form a solid base and can evoke peace or stability. A **diagonal line** moves at a slant. It can shape the rise of a mountain peak or outline a rooftop.

Martin Ramirez. *Untitled (Horse and Rider),* 1954. Pencil, tempera, and crayon on collaged paper, 35 by 58¾ inches. Collection of Jim Nutt and Gladys Nilsson. Photograph courtesy of the Phyllis Kind Gallery, New York.

Look at the curved, straight, and wavy lines Martin Ramirez used in his drawing. What kinds of lines did he use to draw the horse and rider? Where did the artist use horizontal, vertical, and diagonal lines?

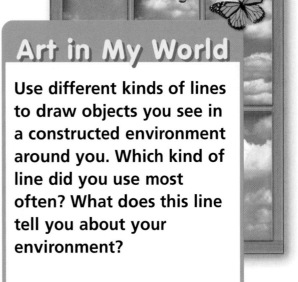

Art in My World

Use different kinds of lines to draw objects you see in a constructed environment around you. Which kind of line did you use most often? What does this line tell you about your environment?

Make a Line Drawing

On a brown paper sack, make a line drawing of an animal and a human rider. Use a variety of lines.

1 Make a large, simple line drawing of an animal.

2 Use horizontal, vertical, diagonal, and curved lines to create the basic shape.

Technique Tip

Use light pressure as you draw to create thin lines. Apply more pressure to create thicker lines.

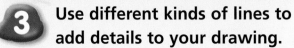

3 Use different kinds of lines to add details to your drawing.

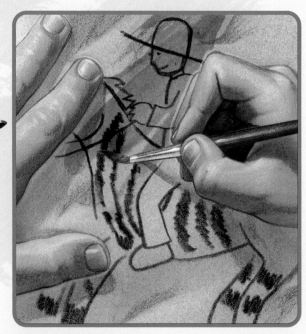

4 Use thinned tempera to paint over your drawing.

Think Like an Artist

How did the different kinds of lines help you add interest to your drawing?

Line and Design

Lines help define objects found in artworks and in natural and constructed environments. An **actual line** can be seen. Look for actual lines in the drawing by Pieter Brueghel. **Implied lines** cannot be seen. They are suggested by other lines, shapes, and colors. Your imagination helps you know where they are.

Pieter Brueghel, the Elder. *Painter and the Patron (with Brueghel's self-portrait),* ca. 1566. Pen and ink drawing, 8⅔ by 10¼ inches. Graphische Sammlung Albertina, Vienna, Austria. Photograph by Erich Lessing.

Which lines in this drawing can you actually see? Which ones are imagined?

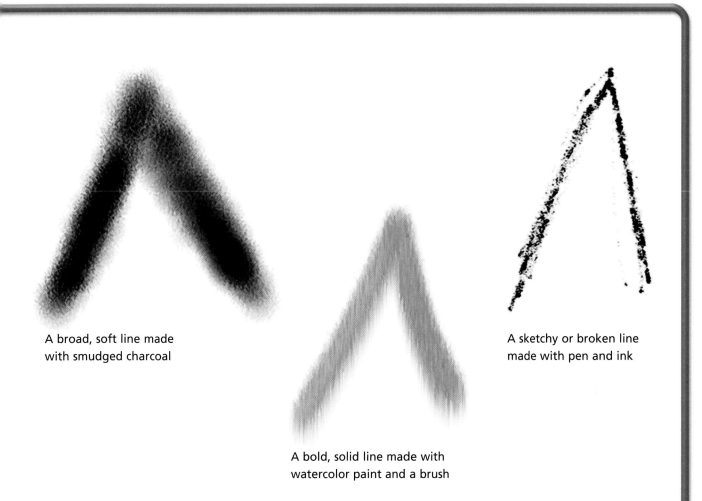

A broad, soft line made
with smudged charcoal

A bold, solid line made with
watercolor paint and a brush

A sketchy or broken line
made with pen and ink

A **design** is a plan for arranging the elements in an artwork. What kinds of lines did Brueghel use in his design for *Painter and the Patron?* Where did he use implied lines?

Artists use a variety of **media,** or art materials, to create certain effects in a design. Brueghel made this drawing using pen and ink on paper. In a watercolor or charcoal drawing of the same subject, the artist might have used more implied lines in the design.

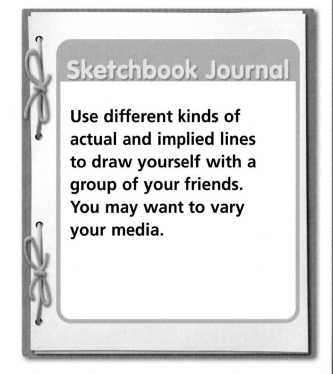

Sketchbook Journal

Use different kinds of actual and implied lines to draw yourself with a group of your friends. You may want to vary your media.

Create Implied Lines

Follow the steps to design a new machine. Use implied lines in your drawing.

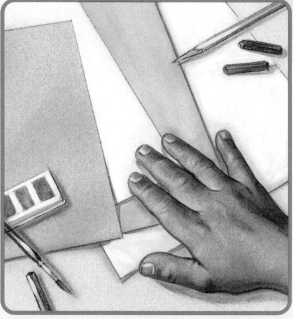

1 Design a new machine that will help you with one of your daily chores.

2 Choose a sheet of colored construction paper for your background.

Technique Tip

Use your finger to smudge, soften, or blend some of the charcoal lines.

3 Use charcoal to draw your design. Include both implied and actual lines.

4 Write a label and caption to identify your machine and describe how it works.

Think Like an Artist

Why did you choose to design this type of machine?

Circus Life

Georges Seurat. *The Circus,* 1890–1891. Oil on canvas, 72⅝ by 59½ inches. Musée d'Orsay, Paris, France.

No two artists see an environment in exactly the same way. Both of these views of the circus were painted in France in the late 1800s. Compare how these two artists saw the circus.

Suzanne Valadon. *The Circus,* 1889. Oil on fabric, 23½ by 19³⁄₁₆. © The Cleveland Museum of Art, bequest of Leonard C. Hanna, Jr., 1958.56.

Look at the lines the artists used. Think about the feelings that each artist wanted to communicate. Which painting best matches the feelings you have about the circus? Explain your answer.

Sketchbook Journal

Plan a design for a painting to show your view of a circus. Describe details you would add. How does your design compare to the artworks on these pages?

Balance

Artists use a principle of design called balance. **Balance** is the way parts of a design are arranged.

Artworks that show **symmetry** look about the same on both sides. Many things in nature, such as butterfly wings or leaves, show symmetrical balance. What makes the carved brackets an example of symmetrical balance?

Artist unknown, Pueblo. *Triangular Carved Bracket*, 1775–1776. Wood, gesso, pigment, 11½ by 9½ by 1¼ inches. Brooklyn Museum of Art, Brooklyn, NY.

Utagawa Hiroshige. *Suido Bridge and Surugadai, No. 48* from *One Hundred Famous Views of Edo,* 1857. Woodblock color print, 14¼ by 9¼ inches. Brooklyn Museum of Art, Brooklyn, NY.

Artist unknown, Aztec. *Feather Fan,* ca. 1550. Mosaic, feathers, and wicker. Museum fuer Voelkerkunde, Vienna, Austria.

Artworks that have sides arranged differently show **asymmetry.** One side carries more weight than the other side. What makes the print of the fish kites an example of asymmetrical balance?

Radial balance shows lines or shapes that spread out from a central point. The petals of a daisy or spokes on a wheel show radial balance. Where do you see an example of radial balance on the feather fan?

Sketchbook Journal

Draw a natural object that shows symmetrical balance. Draw a human-made object that shows asymmetry. Then draw an object that shows radial balance.

Plan an Art Car Design

Follow the steps to design an art car. Use what you have learned about balance to help you.

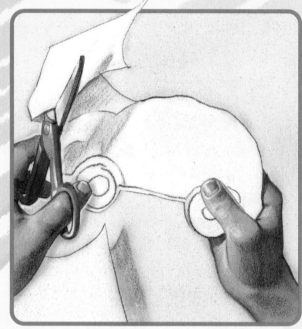

1 Draw an outline of a car. It can be old-fashioned or futuristic.

2 Cut out your car design. Select small found objects to add detail to your car.

Technique Tip

Place your car on a paper plate or piece of cardboard so that you can pick it up and move it before it is dry.

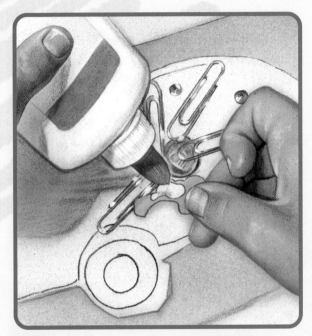

3 Glue down objects to create a balanced design.

4 Add other details that show balance.

Think Like an Artist

Balanced designs make you feel that the elements have been placed just right. What is pleasing about your balanced design?

Lesson 5

Shape

A line may be used to outline a shape. **Shape** is an element of art. It is a flat, two-dimensional area that has height and width. A shape may have a clear boundary, or it may be identified by its area.

A regular shape, such as a square or triangle, is a **geometric shape.** An irregular, free-form shape, such as a cloud, is an **organic shape.** Organic shapes are found in the natural environment.

Harriet Powers. *Pictorial Quilt,* 1895–1898. Pierced, appliquéd and printed cotton, 69 by 105 inches. Museum of Fine Arts, Boston.

Artist unknown, Tlingit. *Dancing Blanket,* 19th century. Mountain goat wool and cedar bark, 52½ by 64 inches.

The way an artist chooses to arrange the parts of an artwork is called **composition.** An artwork's composition creates or conveys certain ideas or feelings.

Look at the panels of the story quilt. Do you like the way Harriet Powers combined types of shapes? Tell why or why not.

Look at the shapes in the Tlingit blanket. What figure do you think might be in the center? How does the artist's composition draw attention to that figure?

Sketchbook Journal

Think about the moon, planets, stars, and constellations. Use geometric and organic shapes to draw these objects seen in the night sky.

Make a Quilt Design

Think about family events and branches of your family tree. Follow the steps to design a family quilt patch.

1 Choose several colors of construction paper to create a quilt block.

2 Cut geometric and organic shapes out of colored paper.

Technique Tip

Use different kinds of lines, such as curved, diagonal, or zigzag, to add details to the designs on your quilt blocks.

3 Glue the shapes onto your quilt block.

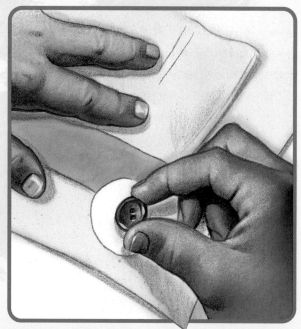

4 Add small sewing objects as details. Combine blocks to make a class quilt.

Think Like an Artist

How do geometric and organic shapes work together in your artwork to make an interesting composition?

Space and Style

The word *space* has a range of meanings, from outer space to parking space to single space. As an element of art, **space** is an area that can be defined by opposites. Space may be empty or full, large or small, positive or negative. Artists use space to communicate ideas.

Space behind and between things is **negative space.** Space filled with the shapes and lines that stand out from the negative space is **positive space.**

Joseph Albers. *Violin Key 7 and 8,* 1935. Gouache, each 14¼ by 8 inches. Josef Albers Museum, Bottrop, Germany.

Josef Albers experimented with how people see color. What color is the negative space in *Violin Key 7 and 8?* Compare the two versions of the painting. What feelings do the two figures give you? Look at *Work—Yellow.* What color is the positive space?

Every artist develops a **style,** or special way of expressing his or her ideas. Paying attention to style can help you recognize an artist's work.

Sketchbook Journal

Draw a picture of an object from the natural environment. Show both positive and negative space. What colors will you use? How will they help show positive and negative space?

Create Negative Spaces

Follow the steps to show negative spaces made by everyday objects.

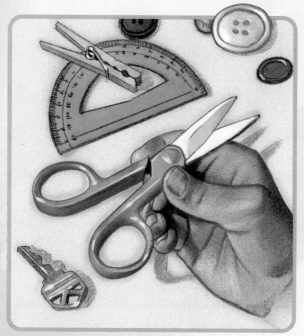

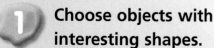 **Choose objects with interesting shapes.**

2 **Choose a position for each object on a sheet of drawing paper.**

Technique Tip

Draw objects more than once to make side-by-side or overlapping images.

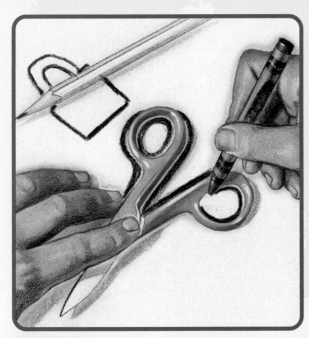

3 Use a black crayon to draw each object.

4 Use oil pastels to color in the negative spaces around the objects.

Think Like an Artist

What space appears more dominant in your artwork, the positive or the negative space? Why?

Garden Landscapes

Barbara Ashmun is an artist, but her medium is plants rather than paints. Ashmun designs gardens for pleasure or picnics or play. Sometimes she plants flowers to attract certain birds. Sometimes she plants fruit and vegetable gardens for food. Once she knows how a garden will be used, she creates a space that is both beautiful and useful.

How does Ashmun use her palette of plants? She uses flowers, leaves, and bark as a painter would use paint. "I think of the flowers as little dabs of color," she says. "And leaf colors can include a range of golds, silvers, purples, and greens." She also considers how light and shadow will mix with the plants' colors and shapes. She even thinks about how the sunlight changes with the time of day and time of year.

Look around the natural environment. Notice the different colors and shapes that a garden designer has to work with. What kinds of growing art can *you* imagine?

Barbara Ashmun grows her own works of art.

Barbara Ashmun's garden in Portland, Oregon

Draw with Dots

Use dots to draw a scene of the natural or constructed environment around you. Think about how you will use line, balance, shape, and space in your composition.

1 Use a marker to outline the shapes in your scene. Leave the space inside the shapes blank.

2 Include details that show the season and the time of day.

3 Use colored markers or oil pastels to make dots to fill in the positive and negative spaces.

4 You may use more than one color to fill in a shape. Overlap dots of color to create a new color.

Courtney, Age 9. *Horses Under the Sun.* Markers.

Look at how these students balanced the shapes and varied the dots to color the positive and negative space in their scenes.

Allison, Age 9. *Summertime in the City.* Markers.

Share Your Art

1. Identify geometric and organic shapes in your design. Describe where you showed positive and negative space.

2. Describe the color combinations you used when making the dots. Explain which were most effective.

3. Explain how you used the elements of line, shape, and color to convey a certain mood.

Think About Art

Read the art words. Then look at the photographs to find one or more examples of each word.

positive space	line	shape
constructed environment	balance	symmetry

Write About Art

Plan a painting of your local environment. Write about the feelings you want to communicate and the details that you will include in your composition to convey your ideas.

Talk About Art

- Look through your Sketchbook Journal and portfolio.
- Choose your favorite artwork.
- Tell a friend why you like it.
- Describe how you would explore this technique in another composition.

John Biggers. *Family of Five*, 1985. Conte crayon, 24 by 18 inches.
Courtesy of the artist.

Put It All Together

1. How does the artist use line, space, and balance in this composition?

2. Does this artwork show symmetry? Explain your answer.

3. What details from the constructed environment add special meaning to this composition?

4. Which person shown in this artwork would you most like to talk to? Why?

Alma Gunter. *Dinner on Grounds,* 1979–1980. Acrylic on canvas, 24 by 18 inches. Billy R. Allen Folk Art Collection. African American Museum, Dallas, TX. Gift of Mr. and Mrs. Robert Decherd.

Unit 2

Expression and Art

Throughout history, artists have recorded their impressions of people, places, and events. Sometimes artists show an event from the past that is important to them. What type of event did Gunter show in *Dinner on Grounds?* What details set this scene in a particular time and place?

Meet the Artist

Alma Gunter used her sketchbook to draw scenes from her childhood. However, her busy life did not give her much time to paint. When she took up painting later in her life, she recreated her long-ago memories. What does this painting tell you about her childhood? As you read this unit, look for another memory painted by Alma Gunter.

Pattern and Rhythm

A **pattern** is the repeated use of an element, such as color, line, or shape. Some patterns create a feeling of motion, or **rhythm,** in an artwork. Both pattern and rhythm are principles of design. What patterns do you see in the painting on this page? Point out lines and shapes that show rhythm.

Henri Matisse. *Christmas Eve (Nuit de Noël. Nice-Cimiez),* 1952. Gouache on paper, cut and pasted, 127 by 53½ inches. The Museum of Modern Art, New York.

Marcel Duchamp. *Nude Descending a Staircase, No. 2,* 1912. Oil on canvas, 58 by 35 inches. Philadelphia Museum of Art, Philadelphia, PA.

Think of a person going down a flight of stairs. Can you sense the rhythm that goes with this action?

Duchamp captured the rhythm of a person going down stairs in an **abstract** way. The person is shown with simple lines and shapes and does not appear realistic. The artist included only those lines and shapes that seemed most important to the movement of the figure. How did the artist use elements of art to help show rhythm and movement?

Sketchbook Journal

Many types of fabric have patterns. Draw an outfit you imagine that shows pattern. What colors, lines, shapes, or combination of these elements will your pattern include?

Create a Collage

A **collage** is made by gluing paper, pictures, fabric, or other materials to a flat surface. Create an abstract collage using colored paper shapes. Follow these steps.

1 Plan a simple design for your abstract collage. Include pattern and rhythm.

2 Cut out the shapes you need from colored construction paper.

Technique Tip

To cut out more than one "copy" of a shape, cut through two or three layers of construction paper at the same time.

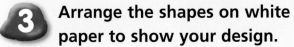
3 Arrange the shapes on white paper to show your design.

4 Glue your shapes to the white paper.

Think Like an Artist

What elements show pattern in your collage? Which patterns create rhythm?

Facial Proportions

Many artists observe a person or groups of people as subjects for artworks. A **portrait** is an artwork that usually focuses on the face. Portraits may show people or animals.

Portraits provide visual records of history and culture. What does this portrait tell you about the people and their culture?

Richard Lindner. *Sunday Afternoon,* 1954. Graphite and watercolor on paper, 25 by 19 inches. Collection of Whitney Museum of American Art, New York. Purchase, with funds from the Friends of the Whitney Museum of American Art. Photography by Sandak, Inc.

This portrait shows a frontal view of the father and son. The mother is shown in profile.

Albrecht Dürer. *Self-Portrait at Age 28,* 1500. Oil on wood, 26⅛ by 19⅛ inches. Alte Pinakothek, Munich, Germany.

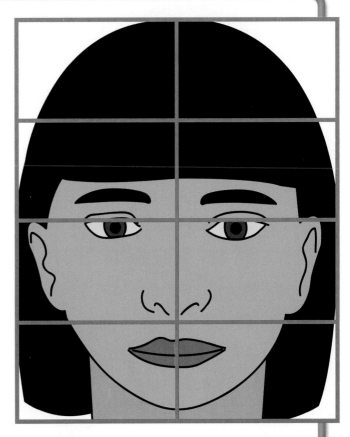

General guidelines like these help artists with facial proportions.

In a **self-portrait,** the artist is the model. Dürer painted himself wearing a fur-trimmed coat. What does this self-portrait tell you about the artist?

Artists often use proportion to place the facial features in a portrait. **Proportion** is the size or placement of something in relation to another thing. This principle of design helps portrait artists make sure the eyes are not larger than the nose, for example, or that the mouth is the right distance between the nose and chin.

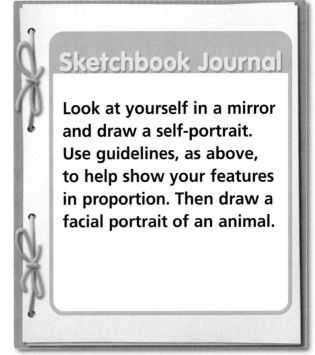

Sketchbook Journal

Look at yourself in a mirror and draw a self-portrait. Use guidelines, as above, to help show your features in proportion. Then draw a facial portrait of an animal.

Draw a Face Portrait

Follow these steps to create a portrait of a classmate. Show a frontal or profile view of your model.

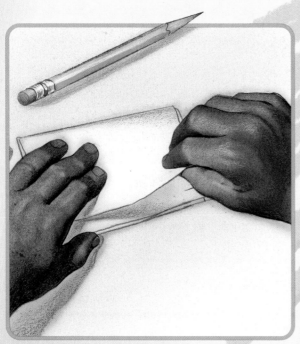

1 Fold a sheet of paper in half. Then fold it in half the other way, then in half again.

2 Draw your model lightly with a pencil first.

Technique Tip

Place the eyes at about the halfway point between the top of the head and the tip of the chin. Notice that everyone has different proportions.

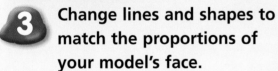 Change lines and shapes to match the proportions of your model's face.

4 Use oil pastels or crayons to finish the portrait. Fill in shadows with dark colors.

Think Like an Artist

How did the guidelines help you make your portrait more accurate?

Space

Thomas Cole placed an old tree in the foreground of this outdoor scene, or **landscape.** The tree appears closest to the viewer. What seems farthest away, or in the background?

Thomas Cole. *View From Mt. Holyoke, Northhampton, Massachusetts, After a Thunderstorm—The Oxbow,* 1836. Oil on canvas, 51½ by 76 inches. The Metropolitan Museum of Art, New York.

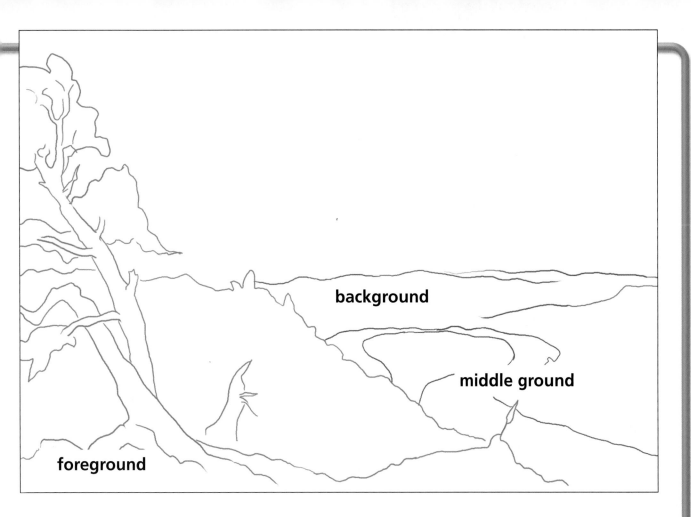

background

middle ground

foreground

The middle ground falls between the foreground and the background. What is in the middle ground of Cole's painting?

Artists can show space and distance by **overlapping** objects. They place objects or shapes in front of others. The object in front appears closer than the object behind it. Notice how the tree in the foreground overlaps other objects in Cole's painting.

Where else do you see objects overlapping in this painting? Which objects appear closer to you?

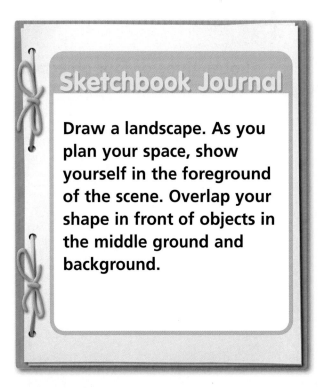

Sketchbook Journal

Draw a landscape. As you plan your space, show yourself in the foreground of the scene. Overlap your shape in front of objects in the middle ground and background.

Studio 3

Draw from Observation

Draw items arranged on your desk. Use overlapping to show the foreground, middle ground, and background.

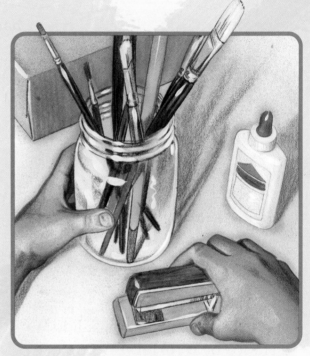

1 Choose three or four objects for your drawing.

2 Place the objects so that one is near, one is in the middle, and one is farther away.

Technique Tip

Instead of drawing the objects, draw the shapes of the objects first. Then fill in the details.

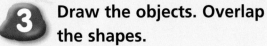
3 Draw the objects. Overlap the shapes.

4 Add color with oil pastels or crayons.

Think Like an Artist

How does overlapping show foreground, middle ground, and background in your artwork?

Seasonal Games

Alma Gunter. *Twilight Games*, 1979. Oil on canvas, 16 by 20 inches. African American Museum, Dallas, TX.

Artists use their artworks to express ideas about the world in which they live. These artworks show children playing. Do the artists seem to share similar ideas about how children play? Explain your answer.

Grandma Moses. *December,* 1943. Oil on pressed wood, 18½ by 21¾ inches. Grandma Moses Properties Co., New York.

Look at how both artists used the middle ground. The fence in *Twilight Games* and the bridge in *December* help focus your attention on the action in the foreground. Describe what is taking place in each painting. Which game would you most like to join? Tell why.

Sketchbook Journal

Make sketches of a summer landscape and a winter landscape. Show you and your friends playing games in each sketch. Use pattern and rhythm to show movement.

Say It with Color

Artists use color to express moods and feelings. How did Cassatt use the **primary colors** of red, yellow, and blue in this drawing? Mixing two primary colors makes a **secondary color.** Find the secondary colors on the color wheel. To make an **intermediate color,** mix a primary and a secondary color. What intermediate colors did Cassatt show in this portrait?

Mary Cassatt. *At the Theatre (Woman in a Loge),* ca. 1879. Pastel on paper, 21¹³⁄₁₆ by 18⅛ inches. The Nelson-Atkins Museum of Art, Kansas City, MO.

Neutral colors include black, white, and gray. Mixing black and white creates variations of gray. Many artists consider brown a neutral color as well. To mix brown, blend two colors that are opposite each other on the color wheel. Neutral colors, like those in the photograph below, often bring about a peaceful or calm mood. How might you use color to express moods in *your* artworks?

Color Wheel

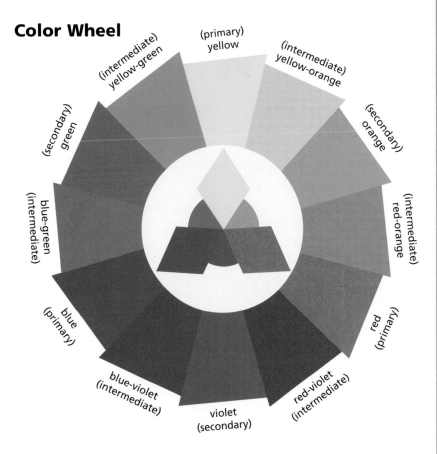

(primary) yellow

(intermediate) yellow-orange

(secondary) orange

(intermediate) red-orange

red (primary)

red-violet (intermediate)

violet (secondary)

blue-violet (intermediate)

blue (primary)

blue-green (intermediate)

(secondary) green

(intermediate) yellow-green

Sketchbook Journal

Use black, brown, white, and gray crayons to create a drawing with light and dark neutral colors. As you draw, think about the light and dark areas you want to show.

Studio 4
Draw with Wet Pastels

Find out what activity a friend likes to do. Then follow these steps.

1 Draw a pencil sketch of a friend doing a favorite activity.

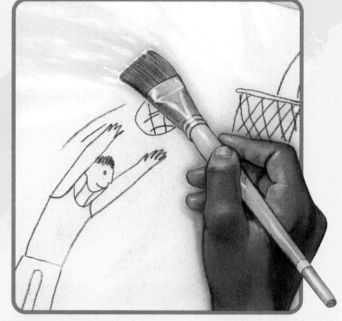

2 Brush or sponge the paper lightly with water.

Technique Tip

Dip your chalk pastel in water to keep it wet when blending colors. Use a dry paintbrush to soften the edges of shapes.

3 Use colored chalk pastels on the damp paper to follow your pencil lines.

4 Fill in the spaces. Blend colors to make secondary and intermediate colors.

Think Like an Artist

What colors did you create as you filled in the shapes in your drawing?

Value

Where do you see lighter and darker blues in *Listening*?
The lightness or darkness of a color is its **value.** A **tint** has a
light value created by adding a dab of color to white. A **shade**
has a dark value created by adding a dab of black to a color.

Gabriele Münter. *Listening,* 1909. Oil on cardboard, 19⅞ by 26½ inches. Städtische
Galerie im Lenbachhaus, Munich. © 1996 Artists Rights Society (ARS), New York/VG
Bild-Kunst, Bonn.

70

Marsden Hartley. *Yliaster (Paracelsus),* 1932. Oil on paperboard, mounted on particle board, 25¼ by 28½ inches. Smithsonian American Art Museum, Washington, D.C.

Look at the tints and shades that Marsden Hartley used in this painting. Point to a spot where a tint is right next to a shade. Notice how the contrast makes the shapes stand out.

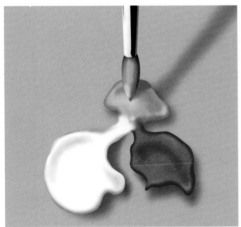

What would you call this tint of red?

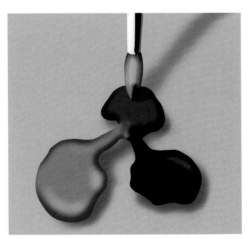

What is the result of mixing a little black with blue?

Sketchbook Journal

Mix white and black crayons or oil pastels with other colors to create a variety of tints and shades. You can also let the white paper show through the colors to create tints.

Paint with Color Values

Use tints and shades to paint a picture of a round object, such as a ball.

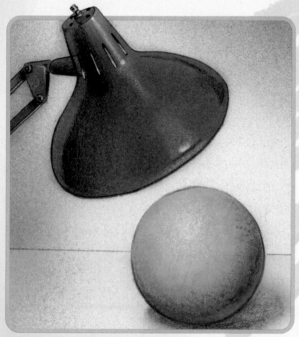

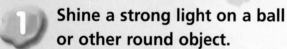 **1** Shine a strong light on a ball or other round object.

2 Choose a color to paint your picture of the round object.

Technique Tip

Look carefully at the light and dark areas that the light creates on the round object. Then recreate the shapes of those areas on your painting.

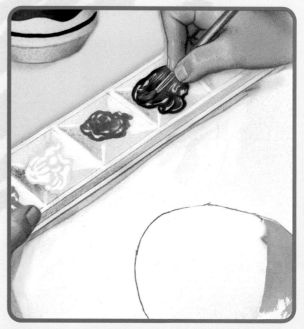

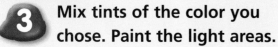
3 Mix tints of the color you chose. Paint the light areas.

4 Mix shades of the color you chose. Paint the dark areas.

Think Like an Artist

Compare your painting to your classmates' paintings.
Identify where the light source is in each painting.
Find the shadows.

Color Schemes

A **color scheme** is a plan for combining colors in a work of art. Artists use different color schemes to create different effects. Each of these views of an armchair shows a different color scheme. Each one can convey different feelings or moods.

A monochromatic color scheme shows shades and tints of only one color.

An analogous color scheme shows colors that are beside each other on the color wheel.

A complementary color scheme shows colors that are opposite each other on the color wheel.

In addition to color schemes, color groups, or families, help artists express ideas in their artworks. Reds, oranges, and yellows are **warm colors.** They may remind you of heat, fire, or warmth from the sun.

Blues, greens, and violets are **cool colors.** They may remind you of cool grass, ice, or refreshing water.

From what color grouping did Matisse choose his colors for this painting? What feeling do you think he wanted to convey?

Henri Matisse. *Large Red Interior,* 1948. Oil on canvas, 57 by 37⅛ inches. Musée National d'Art Moderne, Centre Georges Pompidou, Paris, France.

Sketchbook Journal

Use an analogous color scheme to draw a picture of your home. Then choose a complementary color scheme to fill in the background. When choosing colors, think about what feeling you want to convey.

Studio 6

Plan a Color Scheme

Imagine a perfect room. What mood does it reflect? Follow these steps to paint a monochromatic picture of it.

1 Choose a warm or cool color, depending on the mood of your room.

2 Mix some tints and shades of your chosen color.

Technique Tip

Make shapes stand out by placing tints next to shades. Step away from your painting. Notice how the differences help you see shapes more clearly.

3 Paint objects in the foreground, middle ground, and background.

4 Use different tints and shades to add details.

Think Like an Artist

What mood were you trying to convey with the color scheme you chose? Were you successful? Explain.

Book Illustrations

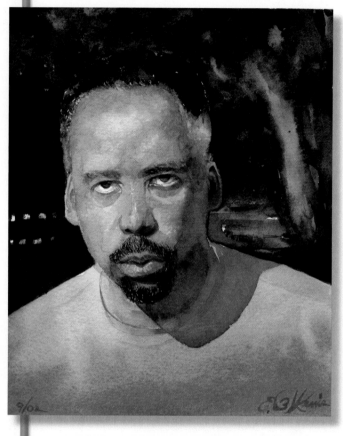

E. B. Lewis.
Self-Portrait, 2003.

time doing research. He travels to the place where the story is set to get a feel for the landscape. He uses photographs of models to create the portraits of the characters. "I go to the region and look for models that have the right character." He says that "a twinkle in the eye or a twist of the lip" can change a person's whole expression. By paying attention to detail, Lewis captures the parts of people that make them special. He brings the story world to life through his interpretation of an author's words.

E. B. Lewis is an artist and educator. He combines his talent for painting with his love of good stories to create beautifully illustrated children's books.

Lewis paints with watercolors. He enjoys painting quickly, without making sketches first. "It allows me to put paint to paper as fast as I can think it," he says.

When he is working on a book, Lewis spends

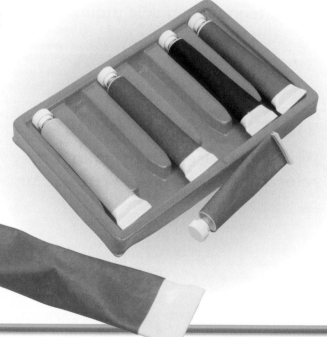

This illustration by E. B. Lewis is from *The Other Side*, by author Jacqueline Woodson.

What is Lewis's color scheme? What mood does it create?

Weave a Paper Mat

Think of warm and cool colors you can use to paint an abstract design that shows pattern and rhythm. Then follow these steps to weave a paper mat.

1 Choose three cool colors. With each color, paint a large spiral, using broken lines. Let dry.

2 Repeat Step 1 on another sheet of paper. Use three warm colors. Paint to the edge of the page.

3 Fold the cool color paper in half. Draw and then cut lines from the fold to one inch from the edge.

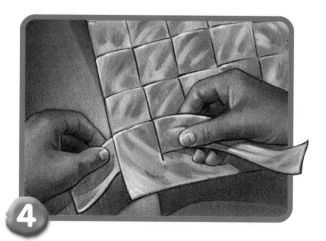

4 Cut the warm color sheet into one-inch strips. Weave these into the cool color strips. Glue edges.

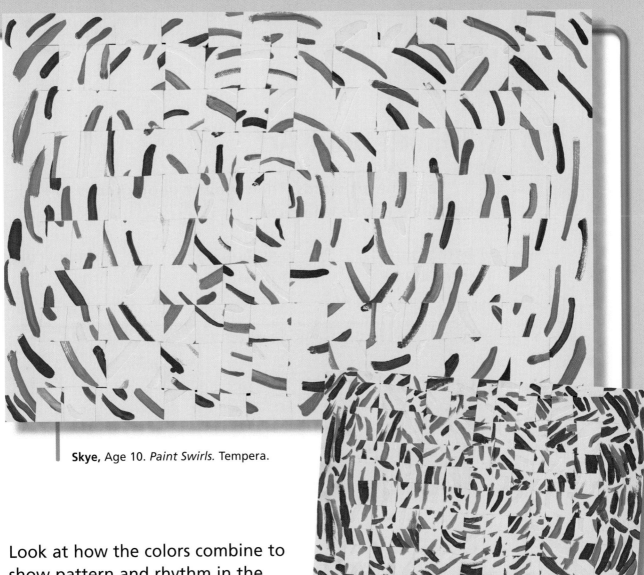

Skye, Age 10. *Paint Swirls.* Tempera.

Breanna, Age 10. *Spiral Design.* Tempera.

Look at how the colors combine to show pattern and rhythm in the mats these students wove.

Share Your Art

1. Identify the warm and cool colors you used.

2. Describe how the warm and cool colors look together. Identify any complementary colors you used.

Think About Art

Read the art words. Then use the photographs to find an example for each word.

background	overlapping	primary color
foreground	proportion	tint

©1990 USPS

Write About Art

Plan a landscape painting. Describe what will be in the foreground, middle ground, and background. Plan the color scheme you will use. Write about how you will use color to convey a certain feeling or mood.

Talk About Art

- Look through your Sketchbook Journal and portfolio.
- Choose an artwork for which you mixed colors.
- Name the colors you used. Tell how you mixed them. Explain why you chose those colors.
- Describe how using different colors would change the artwork.

Peter Hurd. *Eve of St. John,* 1960. Tempera on board, 28 by 48 inches (71 by 121.9 cm). San Diego Museum of Art. Gift of Mr. and Mrs. Norton S. Walbridge. 1975:069.

Put It All Together

1. How did the artist show space in this landscape?

2. What color scheme did the artist use? What effect does the color scheme have?

3. What feeling do you get from looking at this landscape?

4. What are your thoughts about this painting? Explain.

Betye Saar. *Spirit Catcher*, 1976–1977. Mixed-media floor assemblage, 45 by 18 by 18 inches. Collection of the artist.

Art, Past and Present

Art history is the study of how people from different cultures and times express ideas through their artworks. These artworks are found in museums, galleries, and places where they were created. People who study art history identify and interpret symbols. A **symbol** is a color, letter, sign, or picture that has special meaning. What symbols do you see in *Spirit Catcher?*

Meet the Artist

Betye Saar uses old and new objects that she collects to create her three-dimensional artworks. She borrows symbols from different cultures to show connections between people and places. Saar tries to show "cultural differences and universal similarities" in her artworks.

You will find more of Betye Saar's artwork later in the unit. Look for an imaginative form that shows symbols from several different cultures.

Texture

Paintings and drawings are flat. They have two dimensions, height and width. Geometric and organic **forms** are three-dimensional. They have height, width, and depth. You can pick up small forms. You can go around large ones and view them from all sides.

Luis Jiménez. *Vaquero,* 1980. Fiberglass with acrylic urethane finish, height 16½ feet. Courtesy of Luis Jiménez.

Which geometric forms do you recognize?

Which organic forms do you recognize?

For thousands of years, artists have used forms to express ideas about cultures and places. A **sculpture** is a three-dimensional artwork made by carving or joining materials or objects. The materials and methods used to create a sculpture determine its texture. **Texture** is an element of art that refers to the way a thing feels. **Tactile texture** is how a surface actually feels. **Visual texture** is how a surface looks.

What would *Vaquero* feel like if you touched it? What is its visual texture?

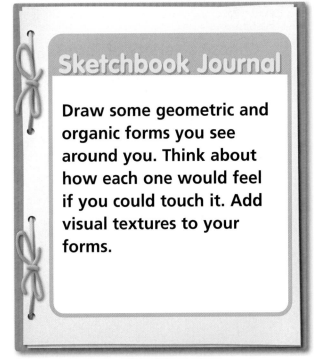

Sketchbook Journal

Draw some geometric and organic forms you see around you. Think about how each one would feel if you could touch it. Add visual textures to your forms.

Sculpt with Texture

Make a sculpture of forms. Add tactile and visual texture to your sculpture. Follow the steps.

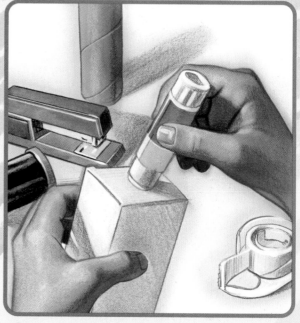

1 Choose a variety of forms, such as paper tubes, spools, or boxes.

2 Attach the forms with glue, staples, or tape.

Technique Tip

Mix a small amount of paint with your glue to add color to your sculpture. Add sand to the glue for some extra visual texture.

3 Brush your sculpture with thinned glue.

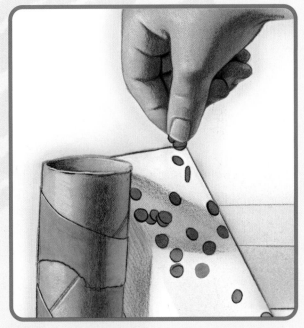

4 Add texture to your sculpture before the glue dries.

Think Like an Artist

What kinds of tactile texture did you add to your sculpture? Does your sculpture have visual texture? Explain.

Emphasis

Elements such as color, texture, shape, and line help draw your attention to a particular part of an artwork. They give importance, or **emphasis,** to that part. What catches your eye in the Kota figure?

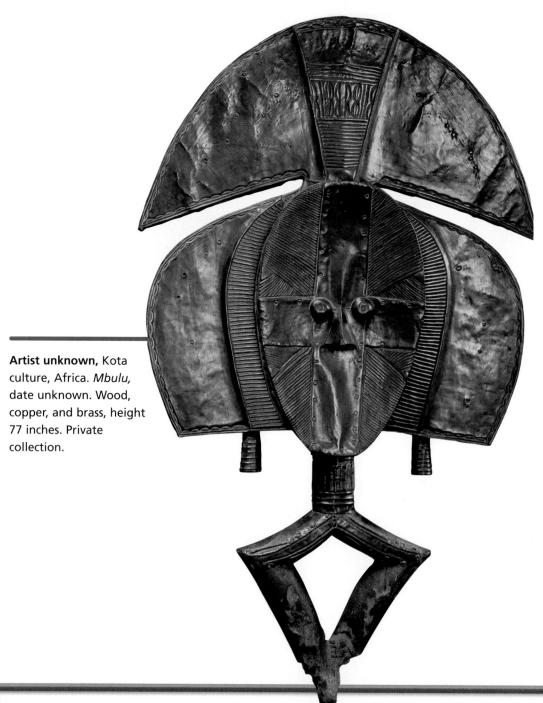

Artist unknown, Kota culture, Africa. *Mbulu,* date unknown. Wood, copper, and brass, height 77 inches. Private collection.

Susan Stinsmuehlen.
Knight Giant, Oil and Wind, 1985. Glass, metals, paint, wood, and mixed media, 27 by 32 inches. Private collection. Photograph courtesy of the artist.

The part of an artwork that gets your attention first is called the **center of interest.** What is the center of interest in *Knight Giant, Oil and Wind?* What element or elements of art did the sculptor use to create emphasis?

Stinsmuehlen's sculpture is an example of **nonobjective** art. It does not represent a particular object that you can recognize. Instead, it conveys a feeling, idea, or cultural symbol.

Art in My World

Go outside and look at forms around you. Find the center of interest in a constructed environment. Draw a picture of it. Show emphasis through your use of one or more elements of art.

Make a Relief Sculpture

In a **relief sculpture,** an image or design stands out from a flat surface. Follow the steps to make your own relief sculpture.

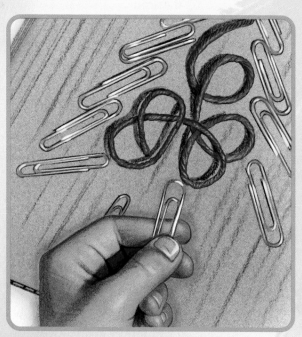

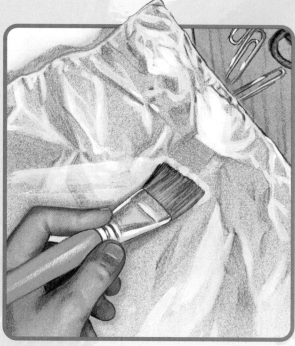

1 Glue objects to cardboard to create a design. Show a center of interest.

2 Brush a sheet of foil with a thin mixture of glue and water. Let it dry.

Technique Tip

Use colored markers to emphasize the relief shapes in the foil.

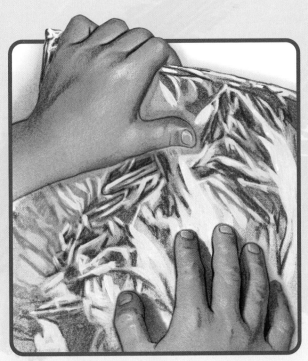

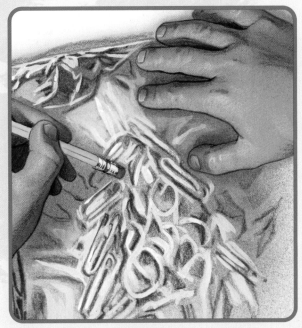

3 Press the foil against the cardboard and fold over the edges.

4 Use a pencil eraser to rub the areas around the raised shapes.

Think Like an Artist

What is the center of interest in your relief sculpture? Describe the elements of art you arranged to show emphasis.

Variety and Subjects

The combination of elements used to create an artwork is called **variety.** Variety is a principle of design that adds interest to an artwork. How do these three chairs, together, show variety?

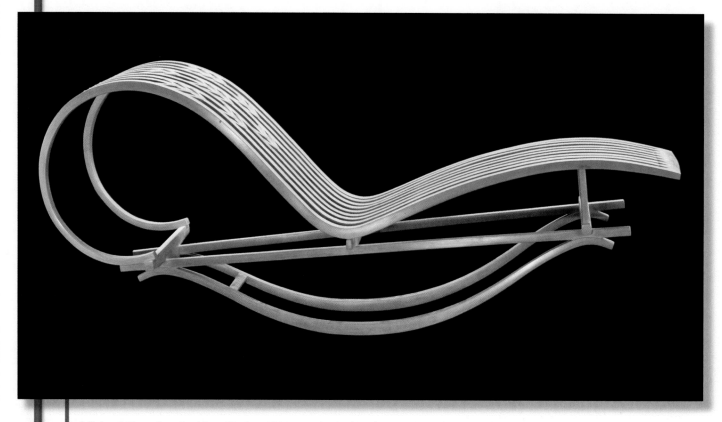

Michael Hurwitz. *Rocking Chaise,* 1989. Laminated mahogany, steel pipe, and yellow ochre milk paint, 36 by 90 by 24 inches. Smithsonian American Art Museum, Washington, D.C.

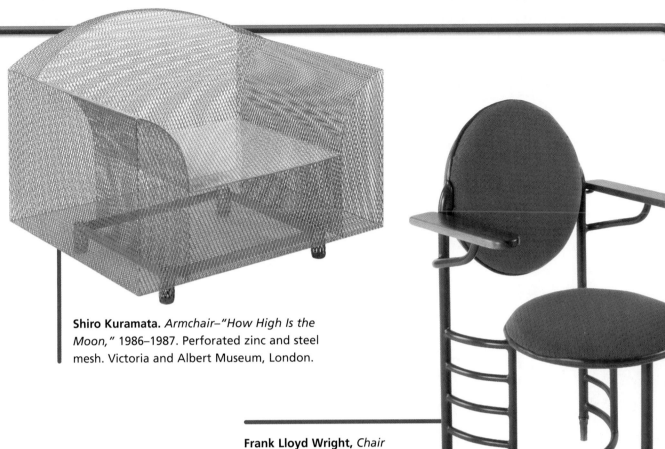

Shiro Kuramata. *Armchair–"How High Is the Moon,"* 1986–1987. Perforated zinc and steel mesh. Victoria and Albert Museum, London.

Frank Lloyd Wright, *Chair Designed for the Johnson Wax Building,* ca. 1939. Metal, wood, and upholstery. Victoria and Albert Museum, London.

The artworks on these pages all have the same subject. A **subject** can be an object, an animal, or a person. What is different about each object?

Think of ideas that different kinds of chairs suggest. A chair can be a place to wait, relax, study, ride, judge, or rule. To plan a chair, an artist might make a **model,** or a small version.

Sketchbook Journal

Consider variety as you create a design for your own model of a chair. Decide what principles of design you will emphasize. Where might you place your chair? How might you use it?

Design a Model

Think of a chair you might see in a science fiction movie.
Follow the steps to make a model of that chair.

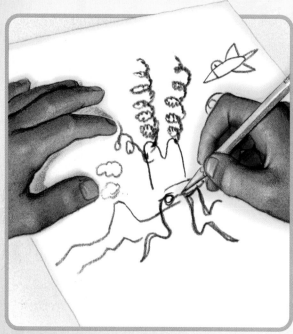

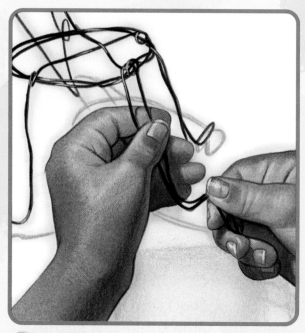

1 Make sketches of a science fiction chair to build.

2 Use wire to make a three-dimensional model of your chair.

Technique Tip

Shape wire by winding it around a pencil to make a coil, or pound it with a hammer to make it flat.

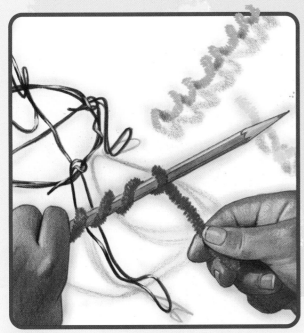

3 Use pipe cleaners and colored telephone wire to add details to your model.

4 Glue fabric, ribbons, string, sequins, and buttons to decorate your model.

Think Like an Artist

Would a chair made from your model be used to sit in or for decoration? Explain.

Temples

Some artists combine images and objects to link their work to other cultures, beliefs, times, and places. How are these two temples alike? How are they different?

Betye Saar. *House of Ancient Memory,* 1989. Wood, paint, plastic, mirrors, embroidered fabric, feathers, metal, glass perfume bottles, painted and lacquered wood table, 61 by 19¾ by 13¼ inches. Collection Walker Art Center, Minneapolis, MN. Butler Family Fund, 1995.

Artist unknown, Indian. *Jagannatha Temple,* ca. 1950. Painted wood, height 19½ inches. Museum of International Folk Art, Santa Fe, NM. Photo by Michel Monteaux.

Look at the two temples again. Compare the variety of elements each artist used to create these special places. What patterns do you see that add interest to each temple?

Think about the ideas that the artists meant to express. Which temple do you think is more interesting? Why?

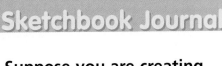

Sketchbook Journal

Suppose you are creating a temple to express an important idea. Give it a title. Write a description of what it would include. Did you combine images and objects from other cultures? Explain the symbols you used.

Ceramic Slab Structures

What medium would you use to make a model of a house? The artist who made *this* model used flat slabs of **clay.** Clay is a powdery substance when it is found in the earth. When it is moistened, it becomes soft. When it is baked, it becomes hard.

Artist unknown, Chinese. *Miniature Funerary House Model,* Han Dynasty. Musée Cernuschi, Paris, France.

What geometric shapes did the artist use?

The art of creating things from clay is called **ceramics.** Some artists, called potters, choose this medium to express themselves.

Potters use different methods to make ceramic artworks. The **slab method** is one way of building objects. First you flatten a ball of clay. Next you cut the parts and score, or scratch, their edges. Then you join the edges with a thin mixture of water and clay called slip. Finally, your teacher bakes, or fires, the hardened clay object in a kiln, or oven.

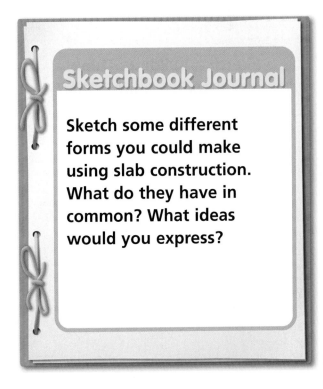

Sketchbook Journal

Sketch some different forms you could make using slab construction. What do they have in common? What ideas would you express?

Build a Slab Structure

Think of a building you would like to design. Use slabs of clay to make a model of the building.

1 Sketch a building. Think about the geometric shapes that make up the building.

2 Flatten a ball of clay. Then roll it out about half an inch thick.

Technique Tip

Before you join the slabs together, gently press small objects into the clay. Remove the objects so their prints create texture on the slab.

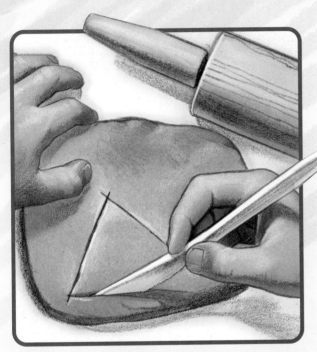

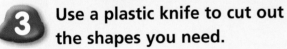 **3** Use a plastic knife to cut out the shapes you need.

4 Score the edges and apply slip. Join the shapes. Paint your model after it is fired.

Think Like an Artist

What geometric shapes did you use to create your model?

Familiar Forms

Bowls have been a part of every culture for centuries. Long ago, all bowls were made by hand. Now, many of them are made by machines in factories. The bowls on these two pages are one-of-a-kind artworks. Artists created them by hand.

Artist unknown. *Painted Bowl with Seven Handles,* Iron Age, II, 1200–1000 B.C. Israel Museum (IDAM), Jerusalem, Israel.

María Montoya Martínez. *Jar,* ca. 1925. Clay with pigments, 11¼ by 12 inches. Eugene and Claire Thaw Collection, Fenimore Art Museum, Cooperstown, NY.

Dale Chihuly. *Golden Yellow Macchia Set with Pale Yellow Lip Wraps,* 1993. Blown glass, 24 by 26 by 26 inches. Collection of the artist.

How are the jar and bowl shown here similar to bowls that were made thousands of years ago?

Dale Chihuly designs bowls of blown glass. The other two bowls are made of clay. Some artists make clay bowls on a pottery wheel. Other artists use the **coil method** and layer snakelike pieces of clay to create the desired shape. A bowl is often **functional.** It has a specific use. A bowl can also be a **decorative** piece to admire and enjoy.

Sketchbook Journal

Make some sketches of a bowl that expresses a cultural influence. Use variety in your design. Will you plan a functional or decorative bowl? How could your bowl be both?

Make a Coil Bowl

Follow the steps to create a clay bowl using the coil method. Will your bowl be functional, decorative, or both?

1 Roll balls of clay into long thin ropes about half an inch thick.

2 Cut a 6-inch round base for your bowl. Attach a coil of clay to the edge.

Technique Tip

Score the top of each coil before going around again. Use slip to attach and smooth each layer as you work.

3 Build the coils upward, joining them by scoring and adding slip.

4 Ask your teacher to fire the bowl. Then glaze it and fire it again.

Think Like an Artist

Compare the shape of your bowl to the bowls your classmates made. What do you notice?

Sculpting Technology

Some artists, like Betye Saar, use symbols of long ago. Other artists show modern times through their materials. What modern objects did this artist use to make these robots?

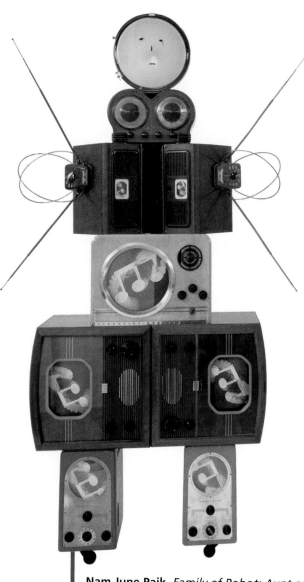

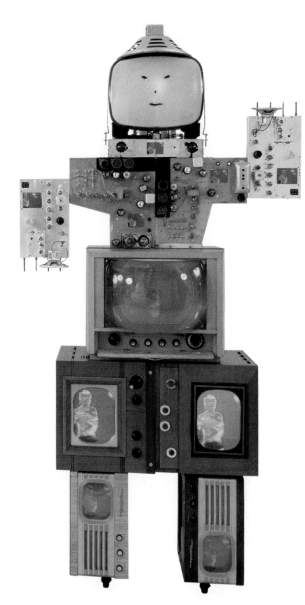

Nam June Paik. *Family of Robot: Aunt and Uncle,* 1986. Vintage television cabinets, vintage chassis, picture tube, paint, video cassette player, video cassette, and television monitors, each approximately 89½ by 45 by 25 inches. Courtesy Carl Solway Gallery, Cincinnati, OH.

This bank of television sets shows a repeated image. What ideas does this give you for a work of video art?

Nam June Paik is a pioneer of **video art technology.** He was one of the first artists to work moving images on television screens into his sculptures. The screens create certain effects that show color, shape, line, and texture. Video clips of movies, advertisements, and television programs appear on the screens to express ideas. How does video art technology reflect the culture you know?

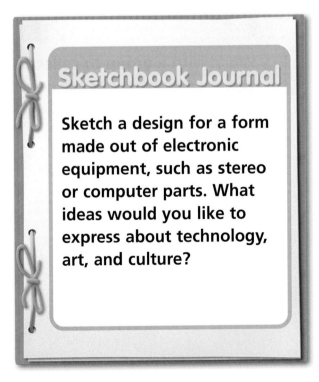

Sketchbook Journal

Sketch a design for a form made out of electronic equipment, such as stereo or computer parts. What ideas would you like to express about technology, art, and culture?

Make a Robot

Make a robot with a message about technology. Follow the steps.

1 Work with a group to collect boxes and cartons you can use to build a robot.

2 Use tape, glue, and wire to put your robot together.

Technique Tip

Put the heaviest part of the robot at the bottom. Or, weight the bottom by placing several bricks or books inside the bottom carton.

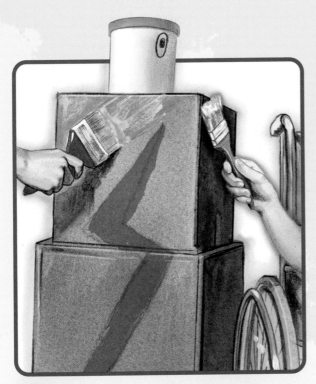

3 Paint your robot and add details using a variety of materials.

4 Decorate your robot with printouts of images you make on a computer.

Think Like an Artist

What message does your group's robot convey about technology? What part do you like best?

Metal Sculptures

Barry George is a sculptor. He does not mold figures of clay or chisel them in stone. Instead, he practices the ancient art of the blacksmith. Using heat to forge metal, George turns his ideas into artwork. The metals he welds together are from the constructed environment. They are everyday things he finds in ordinary places. George watches for lines, shapes, and forms that spark his creativity.

He then uses the objects to build figures. His sculptures reflect his ideas about society and culture. His artworks may be funny or serious, but they are always interesting.

Look around you for bits and pieces of metals. How could you combine these parts to create an artwork? What might they say about your world?

Texas sculptor Barry George says, "I create for my own enjoyment."

Barry George. *Talking Head,* 2001. Steel and found objects, height 24 inches. Collection of the artist.

Create a Sculpture

Imagine yourself playing a musical instrument. Follow the steps to make a sculpture of yourself playing music.

1 Make an armature, or frame, out of straws and pipe cleaners. Show yourself making music.

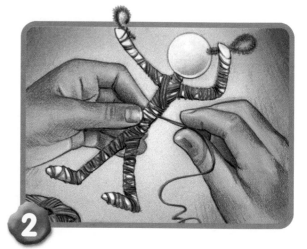

2 Use yarn or masking tape to build up thickness and add details, such as facial features, hands, and feet.

3 Dip thin strips of newspaper into a water and paste mixture. Apply two layers of wet strips.

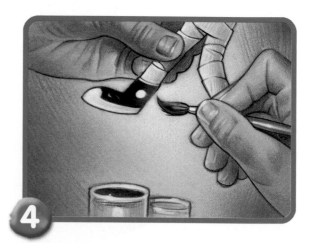

4 When the figure is dry, add color and details with paint.

Paige, Age 11. *Paige with Flute.* Sculpture with papier-mâché and acrylic paint.

Arrington, Age 11. *The Dulcimer.* Sculpture with papier-mâché and acrylic paint.

Notice the variety these students used to create models of themselves as musicians.

Share Your Art

1. Point to the variety of elements you used in your design.

2. Describe how you built the framework for your sculpture. Explain how you overcame the most challenging part of the project.

Think About Art

Read the art words. Then use one or more of the photographs to find an example of that word.

texture
sculpture

symbol
center of interest

functional
ceramic

Write About Art

Plan a sculpture for a community park. Write about the feelings you want to express about your community. Describe what you will add to your sculpture to convey your ideas.

Talk About Art

- Look through your Sketchbook Journal and portfolio.
- Choose a sketch or artwork that shows symbols reflecting your culture.
- Tell a friend what the symbols mean.
- Describe other media that you might use to show symbols and culture in your artworks.

Constantin Brancusi. *The Kiss,* ca. 1912. Limestone, 23 by 13 by 10 inches. Philadelphia Museum of Art, the Louise and Walter Arensberg Collection. © 1997 Artists Rights Society (ARS), New York/ADAGP, Paris. Photograph by Graydon Wood, 1994.

Put It All Together

1. How would you describe the forms and lines the artist used in this sculpture?

2. What element or elements of art did the sculptor use to show emphasis?

3. How does the medium add special meaning to this sculpture?

4. If you were planning a sculpture about feelings and emotion, would you study this sculpture? Explain.

Andy Warhol. *Cow,* 1966. Screenprint, printed on wallpaper, each image 45½ by 29¾ inches. The Andy Warhol Foundation, Inc./Art Resource, NY. © 1998 Andy Warhol Foundation for the Visual Arts/ARS, New York.

Unit 4
Art as Self-Expression

People express themselves in different ways. Some sing. Some write poetry. Visual artists may paint, sculpt, or take photographs. Some artists, such as Andy Warhol, may use a combination of media to express themselves. You, too, may express yourself in a combination of ways. Looking at the media and techniques other people use may give you new ideas about expressing your own ideas, feelings, and beliefs.

Meet the Artist

Andy Warhol began his career as a graphic artist. He also explored painting, sculpture, and filmmaking. Warhol used different media, depending on the message he wanted to convey. You will find another example of Andy Warhol's artwork later in this unit. Look for a familiar image.

Andy Warhol. *Self-Portrait,* 1967.

Pattern

Some artists create original designs to express themselves. Others use designs passed down from one generation to the next. These designs link new ideas to old cultural ties.

Artist unknown, American Indian, Southwest Navajo. *Blanket,* 19th century. Double-faced weave, 76¼ by 52½ inches. Cincinnati Art Museum, Gift of Mrs. C. Gordon Neff. 1937.373.

Today, weavers may use modern tools to follow traditional patterns.

Navajo weavers use color and pattern combinations that are centuries old in the ancient process of making cloth, or **weaving.** To create their designs, weavers use a **loom,** a rigid frame that holds a parallel set of threads, or **warp,** stretched tight. Threads going across the warp are called the **weft.** The weft is pulled over and under the warp to create the designs.

Sketchbook Journal

Draw a blanket design. Use some combination of lines, shapes, and colors to create a pattern. Use crayons and press hard to show strong, bold colors.

Weave a Pattern

Follow the steps to make a loom and create your own weaving patterns.

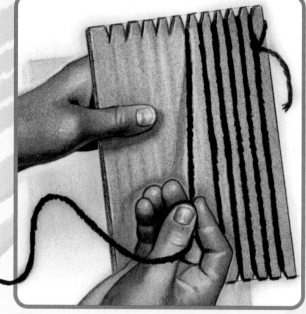

1 Notch the edges at each end of a sheet of cardboard to make a loom.

2 Hook yarn on the first notch then around one at the bottom, then top, and so on.

Technique Tip

Run your weft thread at a 45° angle across the warp and then push it into place with a fork or comb. The edges of your weaving will stay even.

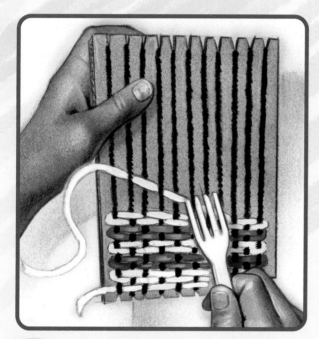

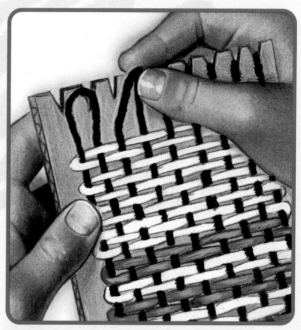

3 Weave the weft over and under the warp threads. Create a pattern.

4 Unhook the warp threads from the loom. Knot the ends.

Think Like an Artist

How did using different colors and textures of yarn help you create your pattern?

Printmaking

Like weavers, printmakers apply ancient techniques to express new ideas. They use ink to transfer an original image from one surface to another. This process is called **printmaking.**

Katsushika Hokusai. *Two Small Fishing Boats at Sea.* Color woodblock print. Musée des Arts Asiatiques-Guimet, Paris.

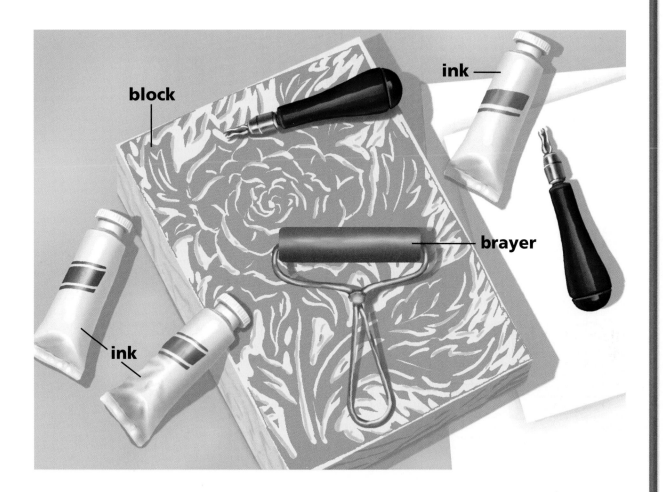

block

ink

brayer

ink

Look at the composition of Hokusai's **print.** To create this **relief print,** the artist carved lines and shapes into a wooden printing **block.** He cut away the surface area not meant to hold ink. This is the negative space. Using a roller called a **brayer,** he then applied ink to the raised areas left on the block. These raised areas appear as positive space on the print. Finally, he pressed paper against the flat surface to "pull a print" of the little boats being tossed in the waves.

Art Fact

Hokusai created thousands of woodblock prints. He found his inspiration in cultural traditions and local landscapes. French Impressionists were later influenced by Hokusai's work.

Create a Relief Print

Think of a special event you have seen or attended. Follow the steps to create a relief print.

1 Make a sketch of an important event. Use paper the same size as a meat tray.

2 Place your best sketch on the meat tray. Go over the lines again with a pencil.

Technique Tip

You may want to add more details to the positive or negative space of your printing block after making your first print.

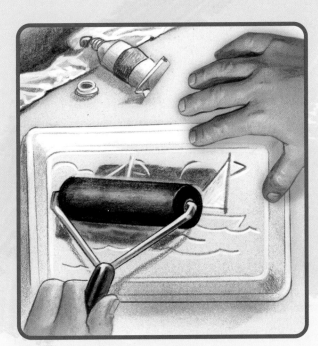

3 Roll a thin layer of ink over the tray with a brayer.

4 Press a sheet of paper over the block. Rub gently. Pull the print.

Think Like an Artist

Did your print turn out like you expected? What will you change when you make another print? Explain.

Unity and Variety

As artists work, they often study other artists. They try techniques and explore new ideas. Little by little, they develop their own distinct styles as they find ways to express themselves. By studying artists' styles, you can recognize their work and identify how they influence others.

Henri Matisse. *The Thousand and One Nights,* 1950. Gouache on cut-and-pasted paper, 54¾ by 147¼ inches. Carnegie Museum of Art, Pittsburgh. Acquired through the generosity of the Sarah Mellon Scaife family, 71.23. © 1997 Succession H. Matisse, Paris/Artists Rights Society (ARS), New York. Photograph by Peter Harboldt, 1994.

Matisse combined symbols and other shapes similar to these to create his collage.

You may be familiar with the bright colors and organic shapes that show Matisse's style. Read the credit line. Compare the size of this large artwork to something in your classroom.

Matisse used cut paper and paint to create a **collage.** He arranged and glued fabrics, paper, or found objects onto a surface. Notice the variety, or combination of elements. The elements work together to create harmony, or **unity.** Variety and unity are principles of design.

Sketchbook Journal

Use line, shape, and color to create some symbols that are meaningful to you. Write a brief explanation next to each sketch.

Create a Collage

Work with a group of classmates to create a collage that tells a story.

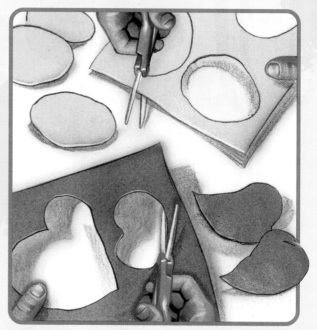

1 Choose a story and design a way to tell it using visual symbols.

2 Cut out your story symbols and arrange them on a large sheet of butcher paper.

Technique Tip

Cut out your symbols without drawing them first to create more original, organic shapes.

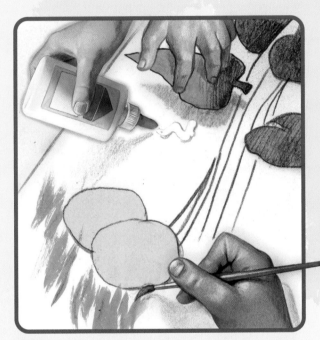

3 Glue down the symbols and use paint to add details.

4 Display your collage and, with your group, tell the story to the class.

Think Like an Artist

What symbols did you choose to tell your story? What meaning do they have? How do the symbols provide variety and unity in your collage?

Look and Compare

Symbols

The Statue of Liberty and the monument to Simón Bolívar stand for freedom and independence. Compare how the artists used the two symbols to express these ideas.

Andy Warhol. *Statue of Liberty,* 1963. Synthetic polymer paint and silkscreen ink on canvas, 80 by 61 inches. Andy Warhol Museum, Pittsburgh, PA.

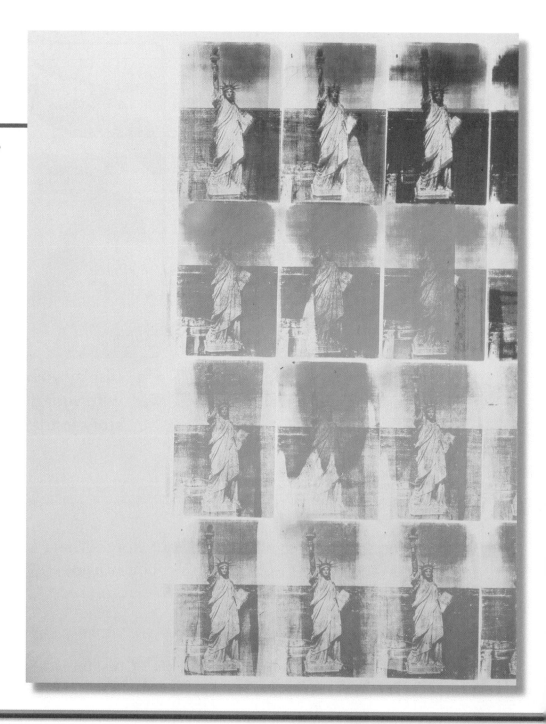

Artist unknown, Peruvian. *Dance Cape: Monument to Simón Bolívar,* 1958. Embroidered fabric with metallic yarns. Girard Foundation Collection. Museum of International Folk Art, Santa Fe, NM. Photo by Michel Monteaux.

Artists use symbols that are meaningful to them. Think about liberties you have and those you look forward to having. Find parts of each artwork that remind you of freedom.

Both of these artworks show unity and variety. Explain how each artist used line, color, and shape to create unity. How did the artists show variety?

Sketchbook Journal

Research the history of the Statue of Liberty and of Simón Bolívar. Draw a symbol that expresses your idea of liberty. Write a short description to explain your meaning.

Artistic Adornment

People may express themselves through the clothing and **jewelry** they wear. Jewelry can be as simple as a plain band of silver or as ornate as this belt buckle. Look at the repeated design, or **motif.** How would the buckle change without a motif?

Artist unknown, Dutch. *Belt Buckle for Day of Atonement,* 1909. Silver: cast, chased and stamped, 2⁹⁄₁₆ by 5¹¹⁄₁₆ inches. Inv.: S1459. The Jewish Museum, New York.

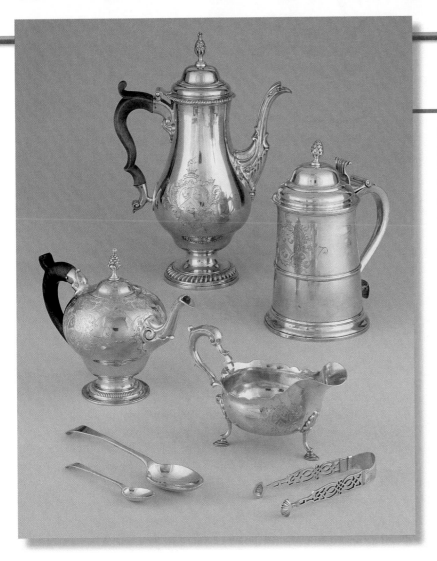

Paul Revere. *Paine Service,* 1773. Silver. Worcester Art Museum, Worcester, MA. Gift of Frances and Eliza Paine, Dr. and Mrs. George C. Lincoln, and Richard K. Thorndike.

Artists often use their skills to make everyday objects, such as a belt buckle, beautiful. An artist whose medium is silver may make cups and serving pieces like those shown here. Paul Revere was an American patriot. He gained fame for his midnight ride, but he was also known for his fine work as a **silversmith.**

Sketchbook Journal

Draw motifs that could be used in a belt buckle design. Think about events or occasions where the buckle can be worn. What other jewelry designs can you draw?

Create a Buckle Design

Follow the steps to create a design for a belt buckle.

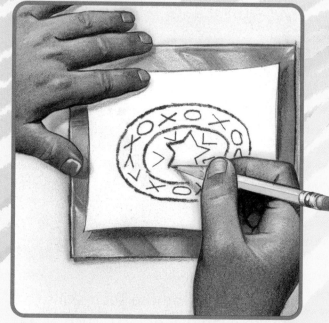

1 Draw a design for a metal belt buckle. Draw simple patterns as a design motif.

2 Transfer your design to a sheet of copper foil.

Technique Tip

Press the foil gently with the pencil eraser. To press small spaces, use a craft stick.

3 Place layers of newspaper under the foil.

4 Use a pencil eraser to press spaces around the shapes in your design.

Think Like an Artist

How did you use texture and pattern to create interest in your belt buckle design?

Industrial Design

Some artists work in **industrial design.** They design everyday objects to be both useful and beautiful. Jazzy cars, interesting clocks, and sleek office supplies are all forms of **functional art.**

Ed "Big Daddy" Roth. *Beatnik Bandit (TM) II,* 1994. National Automobile Museum (The Harrah Collection), Reno, NV.

How does the car's body style complement the engine?

Ordinary objects can be manufactured with a modern or unique style.

Artists who create the designs for factory-made objects are called industrial designers. Many of these artists draw their design plans on computers. Then they create a three-dimensional model of the design. The drawings and models help factory workers make everyday objects with machines.

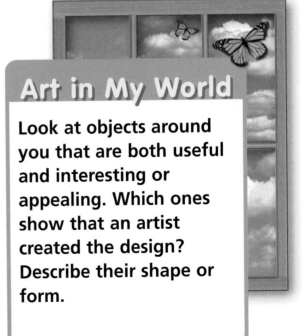

Art in My World

Look at objects around you that are both useful and interesting or appealing. Which ones show that an artist created the design? Describe their shape or form.

Design a Car

Follow the steps to design a car for a cartoon character.

1 Draw a design for a car for a favorite cartoon character.

2 Transfer your design onto a large sheet of paper. Show the cartoon character.

Technique Tip

Consider comfort and safety as you design your cartoon character's car. In addition, how can you add style or beauty to the vehicle?

3 Use markers or paint to color your car.

4 Use your imagination to add details that will make the car one of a kind.

Think Like an Artist

What details make your cartoon character's car both functional and attractive?

Graphic Design

Many of the books, magazines, posters, and advertisements you see include both words and pictures. Artists who work in **graphic design** planned the arrangement of those words and pictures. The book jacket below shows a graphic design using both words and a reproduction of a paper cutout artwork.

Book jacket illustration for the Texas Book Festival program, November 14–17, 2002. Featuring *Flowery Words/Wisdom, Poetry, Song, & History* by Carmen Lomas Garza. Original artwork: white paper cutout, 36 by 28 inches. © 1993 Carmen Lomas Garza.

TEXAS BOOK FESTIVAL

NOVEMBER 14-17, 2002
State Capitol & Colorado Streets, Austin Texas
First Lady Laura Bush, Honorary Chairman

Adrian Avram. *Action,* 2002. Digitally illustrated poster, 16 by 20 inches. Collection of the artist. © 2003 Adrian Avram.

An **illustration** is a drawing that adds meaning to stories and other written information. Illustrations help show things that words cannot explain. You may have seen illustrations in your textbooks. Look at the poster on this page. What could it be illustrating?

Sketchbook Journal

Make sketches for a poster to advertise a local event, such as a fair, a race, or an arts festival. What illustration will you include? What words will you show?

Design a Poster

What message will you design to promote your school?
Follow the steps to create a poster.

1 Think of a message you would like to show on a poster.

2 Cut letters and pictures from magazines to create a slogan and illustration.

Technique Tip

Add details to your poster using cut paper, markers, or paint.

3 Arrange the letters and pictures in an interesting and pleasing way.

4 Glue the letters and pictures onto a sheet of oak tag or heavy paper.

Think Like an Artist

How do your illustrations and design send the message you want to convey?

Museum Exhibitions

When Raquel Aguiñaga-Martinez was in high school, she wanted to be a marine archaeologist. But then she got a summer job at a Chicago museum. It changed her life.

"It sparked my interest and exposed me to a whole different world," says Aguiñaga-Martinez. What began as a summer job became a career. She worked at the museum through college and eventually became a full-time employee. Now she helps plan exhibitions of works by artists from the United States, Mexico, and Canada.

Putting together a show is a team effort. Staff members of the museum help. Aguiñaga-Martinez gets permission to borrow artworks from artists, collectors, or other museums. Then she has to prepare the exhibition space. Carpenters and painters build and paint new walls. Sometimes the group has only a few weeks to remove one exhibition and install a new one.

During the exhibition, museum guides share information with visitors. Other staff members may develop activities to help children appreciate the exhibition as well.

Aguiñaga-Martinez has watched the Mexican Fine Arts Center Museum grow into the largest Mexican art museum in the nation. "The best thing is that it's a continual learning process," she says. "It's like [being in] a classroom. You do have homework but you get paid for it. You get paid for learning."

Raquel Aguiñaga-Martinez enjoys teaching people about Mexican culture.

The Magic of Remedios Varo, June 16, 2000–August 20, 2002. Gallery View. Courtesy of the Mexican Fine Arts Center Museum.

Portfolio Project

Create a Graphic Advertisement

Create an advertisement for an industrial design product, an item of jewelry, or a weaving.

1 Use a magazine or catalogue to find an industrial design product, an item of jewelry, or a weaving.

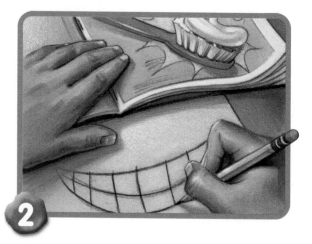

2 Think of the message you want to show in an advertisement. Draw sketches.

3 Use lettering from magazines or use computer graphics to write words for your advertisement.

4 Combine your text with pictures from magazines and your own drawings.

Rachel, Age 9. *Plain as Can Be.*
Collage.

How do the text and pictures
work together to convey a message
in these advertisements?

Caitlin, Age 10. *Pots and Pans.*
Collage.

Share Your Art

1. Explain why you chose the lettering you used.

2. Describe how the letters and pictures work together
to convey the message.

Think About Art

Read the art words. Then use the photographs to find an example for each word.

functional art   illustration   warp
graphic design   industrial design

Write About Art

Plan a classroom gallery show of functional art. Write notes for a brochure about the artworks you will include in the exhibition. Include ideas for graphics that you might use in an exhibition brochure or web page.

Talk About Art

- Choose the technique or type of art that you would like to explore further.
- Describe why you like to express yourself this way.
- Explain to a friend how you could apply this technique or idea to a specific project.

Science & Industry
USA 2Oc

Saul Bass. *Science & Industry,* 1983. U.S. postage stamp, computer-aided design. © United States Postal Service.

Put It All Together

1. What makes this stamp an example of functional art?

2. How does the artist show how science and industry work together?

3. How do the colors reinforce the idea of science combined with industry?

4. Do you like the way the artist expressed his ideas? Explain.

Marc Chagall. *I and the Village,* 1911. Oil on canvas, 75⅝ by 59⅝ inches. The Museum of Modern Art, New York. Mrs. Simon R. Guggenheim Fund. Photograph © 1996 The Museum of Modern Art, New York. © 1998 Artists Rights Society (ARS), New York/ADAGP, Paris.

Unit 5
All Kinds of Art

Artists express themselves through their artworks in a variety of ways. They use various media, color schemes, techniques, and subjects to express their ideas or feelings.

As you read and look at artworks, you are building a repertoire, a collection of art skills and concepts. You will use your repertoire as you view and create new artworks throughout your life.

Meet the Artist

As a boy, Marc Chagall loved to go on walks through the Russian town where he grew up. As an adult, he used artwork to express the beauty he found in the world around him. Chagall combined reality with his imagination to create visual stories about growing up. What does this painting tell you about his life?

As you read this unit, look for another painting by Marc Chagall.

Marc Chagall. *Self-Portrait,* 1959–1968.

Styles and Subjects

All artists express themselves through their art. In the early 1900s, a group of painters began to use simple designs and bold colors to express their feelings about the subjects of their artworks. Their artworks are **Expressionist** in style.

Alexei Jawlensky. *Summer Evening in Murnau,* 1908–1909. Oil on cardboard. Städtische Galerie im Lenbachhaus, Munich, Germany.

How did Jawlensky use complementary colors in this artwork?

Expressionist artists had similar styles, but there was some variation among them. Jawlensky's style, an example of German Expressionism, shows brilliant colors and only a few details. American artist Lee Krasner's style, called Abstract Expressionism, involves techniques such as using bold or sharp brushstrokes.

Both paintings on these pages have outdoor subjects. The subject of an abstract artwork, such as *Milkweed,* may be unrecognizable to the viewer, but it expresses the artist's interpretation of a subject. Why do you think Krasner chose to use an abstract style to express her thoughts and feelings?

Lee Krasner. *Milkweed,* ca. 1955. Oil, paper, and canvas on cotton duck, 82½ by 57¾ inches. Albright-Knox Art Gallery, Buffalo, NY.

Sketchbook Journal

Make an abstract drawing of a plant. Consider using organic or geometric shapes to simplify the drawing. Do you like this style of art? Explain.

Draw a Landscape

Express your own style as you create a landscape. Follow the steps.

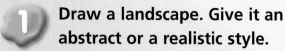 Draw a landscape. Give it an abstract or a realistic style.

2 Include details that describe a place or that show a season.

Technique Tip

Show a foreground, middle ground, and background by overlapping objects in your drawing.

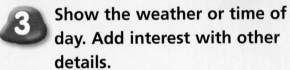

3 Show the weather or time of day. Add interest with other details.

4 Choose a color scheme that expresses your feelings about the scene.

Think Like an Artist

What kind of mood did you express with your landscape? How would you describe your style in this artwork?

Perspective

Artists can make a flat picture appear to have depth or distance. In a drawing or painting, an artist creates **perspective** by using several techniques.

Meindert Hobbema. *The Avenue at Middleharnis,* 1689. Oil on canvas, 40⅓ by 55 inches. The National Gallery, London.

Can you find the road that leads your eye to the center?

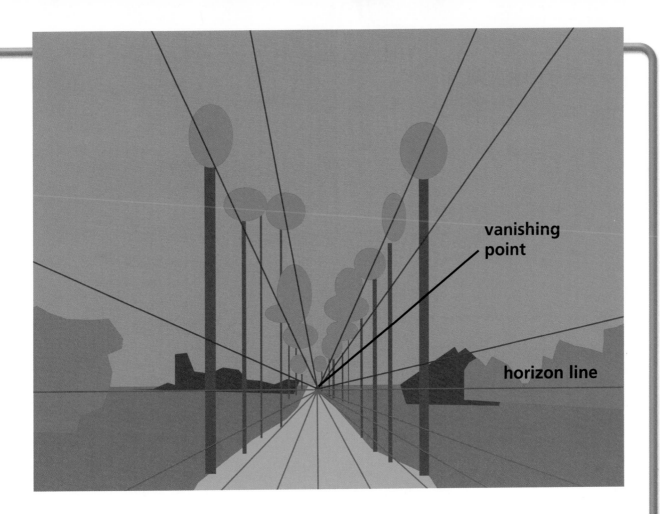

vanishing point

horizon line

Sometimes artists overlap objects to make one appear to be in front of another. Artists may also show objects smaller so they appear to be in the distance. Nearby objects would be larger.

Meindert Hobbema used another technique. Find the straight line where the sky meets the land. This is the **horizon line.** The horizon line meets the road at the **vanishing point.** Notice how the road gets narrower and then vanishes. Is the actual road narrower in the distance? Explain.

Sketchbook Journal

Draw a hallway ending at a doorway in your school or another building. How can you use a horizon line and vanishing point to help arrange your lines? Include a ball or a chair in the foreground and middle ground.

Draw with Perspective

Follow these steps to practice techniques that allow you to show perspective in a drawing.

1 Cut out a picture from a magazine that shows a landscape.

2 Glue the picture onto a larger sheet of paper, leaving a wide border on all four sides.

Technique Tip

Look at the horizon line before you extend it. Is it broken by trees or other objects? If so, allow your extended line to be broken, too.

3 Extend the horizon line. Think about where you might add details.

4 Draw lines from the vanishing point beyond the edges of the picture.

Think Like an Artist

How did the horizon line and vanishing point help you draw with perspective?

Artists as Architects

This **art museum** takes care of artworks for future generations by preserving and displaying them for the public. Some art museums are artworks themselves. They are designed by **architects,** people who plan and arrange buildings and other structures. Architects use the elements of art and principles of design to make their buildings functional and appealing.

Louis Kahn, architect. The Kimbell Museum, Fort Worth, TX.

Interior of The Kimbell Art Museum

The art and science of designing buildings is called **architecture.** Architects first draw a blueprint, or detailed plan, for a building. They may also make a three-dimensional model of the plan. A model helps people see how the building would look.

Landscape architecture involves planning the outdoor spaces around buildings. Landscape architects use plants, trees, walkways, fountains, and other features to add beauty and function.

Sketchbook Journal

Find examples of different roofs and draw them. You may look at the buildings around you and in books or magazines. Why do you think the roofs vary?

Make a Museum Model

Suppose your group's design for a new museum has been chosen. Create a model of your design. Include landscape architectural features as well.

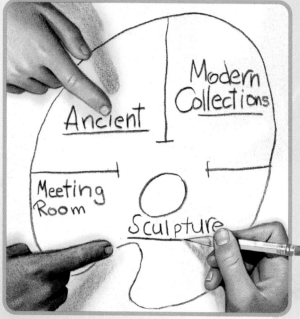

1 Draw a blueprint. Show areas for displays and for activities.

2 Cut forms from paper or tag board for your model. Tape or glue them together.

Technique Tip

Use modeling clay to help secure your model to the base. Clay may also help hold your paper or tag board forms together.

3 Use markers and found objects to add details.

4 Add features to your model to show landscape architecture.

Think Like an Artist

How does the landscape architecture enhance your building? What might visitors say when they come to your museum?

Roosters

Marc Chagall. *The Red Rooster,* 1940. Oil on canvas, 28¾ by 36 inches. Cincinnati Art Museum, bequest of Mary E. Johnston. 1967.1426. © 1998 Artists Rights Society (ARS), New York/ADAGP, Paris.

These artists both showed a rooster in their artworks, yet the media and styles are different. Media, style, and other forms of expression are often influenced by artists' cultures.

Romare Bearden.
Morning of the Rooster,
1980. Collage on board,
18 by 13¾ inches.
Courtesy Estate of
Romare Bearden/ACA
Galleries New York,
Munich.

Romare Bearden's artwork is influenced by his African American culture. He often portrays African American people and reflects the rhythms of jazz and gospel music.

Marc Chagall's artwork reflects his Russian Jewish heritage. Much of his artwork includes fantasy images reflecting his hometown and traditional village life.

Notice how Chagall's painting, as an imaginative image, shows unusual proportions. Discuss how Bearden showed proportion.

Art Fact

Romare Bearden had many interests. He once played semi-professional baseball, drew political cartoons, and earned a college degree in mathematics.

Still Life

A **still life** is an artwork that shows objects that cannot move on their own. Sometimes objects are symbols for ideas. For example, a book might be a symbol for wisdom, or a burning candle might be a symbol for life. What might these roses symbolize?

Pierre-Auguste Renoir. *Roses in a Vase.* Oil on canvas. Christie's, New York.

Artist unknown, Japanese. *Scattered Books*, 17th century. Screen in six parts, painted on goldleaf ground, height 57¾ inches. Musée des Arts Asiatiques-Guimet, Paris.

Many artists use **shading techniques** to give objects depth. Notice the curve of Renoir's vase. He changed values from dark to light, showing light and shadows. As values change, **contrast,** or differences between light and dark, causes certain shapes to stand out from others.

Artists may paint a still life from any side or angle. From what view or angle did Renoir approach his still life? From what angle is *Scattered Books* shown?

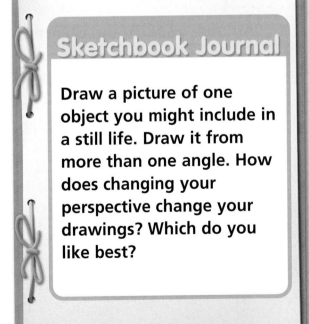

Sketchbook Journal

Draw a picture of one object you might include in a still life. Draw it from more than one angle. How does changing your perspective change your drawings? Which do you like best?

Studio 4
Create a Still Life

Create a still-life drawing of objects or symbols that tell something about you.

1 Arrange your chosen objects on a flat surface. Show balance, emphasis, and unity.

2 Draw the objects from different angles.

Technique Tip

To show a gradual change from light to dark, begin shading with lines or dots far apart and bring them closer together.

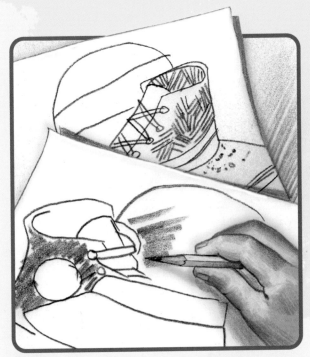

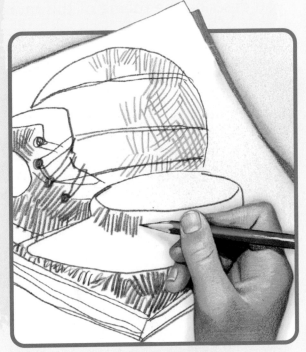

3 Plan where you will use shading techniques to give your objects depth.

4 Create your still life on a large sheet of paper. Use shading to show contrast.

Think Like an Artist

What shading technique did you use to give your objects depth? Were you successful?

Murals

Art that is painted on the surface of a wall or ceiling is called a **mural.** Murals can tell a story, send a message, or add beauty or humor to an otherwise plain surface. How would you describe the theme of this mural?

Malou Flato. (Detail) *Mural,* 1993. Hand-glazed ceramic tiles, 3 panels, each 4½ by 21½ feet. Interior of Central Market grocery store in Austin, TX.

Artist unknown. Mural in Chicago, IL.

Some murals are painted on concrete walls along a freeway or on the outside of a building. Murals may also adorn the ceiling of a church. Sometimes an artist or a group of artists is hired to design and paint a mural.

Malou Flato was commissioned, or hired, to design and create her mural for an interior wall of a grocery store. Notice the glassy texture of the mural. The artist painted the mural on square tiles. She used special **glazes,** or thin liquids made of minerals, that make the clay tiles appear shiny when fired.

What message or story does each mural convey?

Sketchbook Journal

Make a list of themes and images you would include in a mural. Draw a sketch of one subject for your mural. Write about a color scheme and medium you might choose. Tell why.

Make a Mural

Work in a group to design a mural. Consider where you might paint your mural.

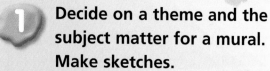 **1** Decide on a theme and the subject matter for a mural. Make sketches.

2 Create a unified composition. Draw a grid of one-inch squares on the drawing.

Technique Tip

Number the squares on your grid and on the cardboard to match. As you fill in each square, match up lines from the squares next to it.

3 On cardboard, draw a grid with six-inch squares. Draw lines to match the original.

4 Use paint or markers to color the mural. Decide where to hang it.

Think Like an Artist

What would you change, if anything, before you painted your mural on a wall or fence?

Mosaics

This mirror was made more than twelve hundred years ago. Its decorative back is a mosaic. A **mosaic** is an artwork made by fitting together tiny pieces of material such as colored glass, tiles, stones, or paper. Artists have been making mosaics for thousands of years.

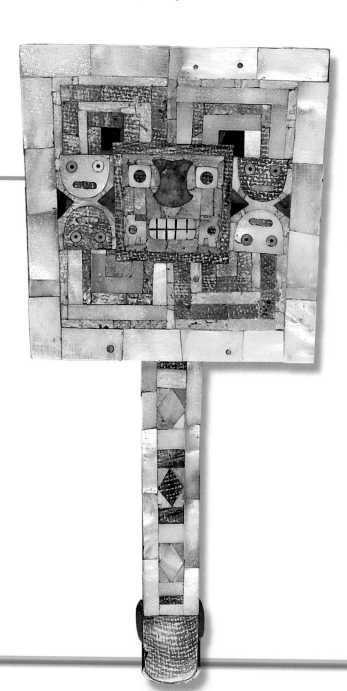

Artist unknown, Central or South coast of Peru. *Mirror,* A.D. 650–800. Mosaic of turquoise, pyrites, and shell, 9½ by 4¾ by ¾ inches. Dumbarton Oaks Research Library and Collections, Washington, D.C.

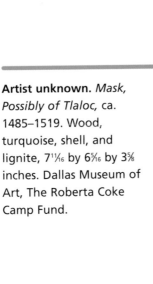

Artist unknown. *Mask, Possibly of Tlaloc,* ca. 1485–1519. Wood, turquoise, shell, and lignite, 7¹¹⁄₁₆ by 6⁵⁄₁₆ by 3⅝ inches. Dallas Museum of Art, The Roberta Coke Camp Fund.

The small materials for mosaics are called **tesserae.** When combined to form lines and shapes, tesserae can become striking artworks.

Look closely at the mask. It was used in ceremonies about five hundred years ago. It is covered with tesserae of colored stone and shell.

How did these artists use balance? Where have you seen a mosaic?

Sketchbook Journal

Draw three sketches showing subjects you would like to show in mosaics. Make a list of found objects and other materials you might include as tesserae.

177

Make a Mosaic

Create a balanced design for a mosaic. Follow the steps below.

1 Select and cut paper tesserae for your mosaic.

2 Draw a large shape for the center of your mosaic on construction paper.

Technique Tip

Work from the center of the large shape outward to help the tesserae fit together well.

3 Spread a small amount of glue. Attach the tesserae.

4 Continue to add glue and colored paper until you have covered your design.

Think Like an Artist

What would you change about your mosaic? What would you keep the same?

Graphic Design

McMillen says, "I always try to do designs that satisfy me—and the funny thing is that they usually end up satisfying the client!"

Who decides where to put the pictures and where to put the text on a page? That is the job of a graphic designer. Nancy McMillen is an art director and graphic designer. As an art director, she hires illustrators or photographers. They create the visuals for a printed work, such as a book, magazine, brochure, or advertisement. An important part of McMillen's job is knowing many skilled artists and photographers to assign to each job.

After illustrations or photographs are sent to McMillen, she begins her work as a graphic designer. She decides how to put the text together with the artwork so the page shows unity, variety, and other principles of design.

McMillen uses knowledge she gained in art school to make decisions about how to attract readers to an article or story. For example, McMillen says, "If a story is about who makes the best hamburger in the state—I might want to use a photograph of a really delicious-looking hamburger. Or, I might decide to have an illustrator do a drawing of the most outrageous, huge, wild-looking hamburger you've ever seen, complete with a blue-ribbon award attached to it."

Look around you. What do you see that must have been planned or produced by a graphic designer?

TEXAS TRAVELER
THE ULTIMATE GUIDE TO THE LONESTAR STATE

Explore the Seven Regions of Texas

Family Day Trips
Ranches ★ Golfing
Shopping ★ Festivals

SUPPLEMENT TO TEXAS MONTHLY

McMillen chose the artwork and designed the layout for this magazine cover.

Make a Still-Life Mosaic

Think of objects you would like to use in an arrangement for a still life. Follow these steps to use the still-life arrangement as a subject of a mosaic.

1 Choose several objects for a still life. Put them in a pleasing arrangement.

2 Draw a sketch of your still-life arrangement on drawing paper.

3 Gather and select tesserae to create a mosaic.

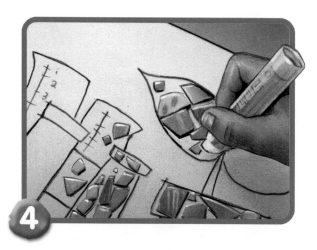

4 Glue down the tesserae. Start from the center of each shape and move outward.

D'Andre, Age 10. *Plant Shelf.* Mosaic.

How did these students use patterns of tesserae to make their still-life mosaics?

Dominique, Age 10. *The Paradise of Beans.* Mosaic.

Share Your Art

1. How closely did your artwork resemble the still-life arrangement of objects?

2. What patterns and colors did you use to create your mosaic?

3. How did you use pattern and color to create shading?

Think About Art

Read the art words. Then use the photographs to find an example for each word.

horizon line
architecture

mosaic
vanishing point

still life
perspective

Write About Art

Plan a painting in an Expressionist style. Describe how you will use shape. Write about how you will use color to convey a certain feeling or mood. How will you use perspective to create depth and distance?

Talk About Art

- Look through your Sketchbook Journal and portfolio.
- Choose an artwork in which you showed perspective.
- Name the techniques you used to give the artwork depth or to show distance. Explain the techniques.
- Describe how using different media would change the artwork.

Wassily Kandinsky. *Romantic Landscape,* 1911. Oil on canvas. Städtische Galerie im Lenbachhaus, Munich, Germany.

Put It All Together

1. Look closely at the artwork. Identify the types of lines the artist used. What kinds of shapes do you see?

2. Which elements of art are emphasized in this artwork? Do you see a horizon line? Explain.

3. What is another title you might give this painting? What makes your title a good choice?

4. Do you prefer a realistic subject or an abstract one? Explain.

Jaune Quick-to-See Smith. *Indian Men Wear Shirts and Ties,* 1996–1997.
Lithograph and pulp painting, 48 by 29 inches. Art Museum of Missoula,
Missoula, MT. © Jaune Quick-to-See Smith.

Unit 6

More Ideas for Art

Artists see the world in new and different ways. They may see an opportunity for a photograph in a mud puddle or imagine a painting from a dream. Some artworks, like this one, show symbols about a culture. Like other artists, this artist draws ideas from memory, observation, and imagination.

Meet the Artist

American artist Jaune Quick-to-See Smith communicates ideas about her Native American culture through her artworks. To make her ideas clear, she includes both words and images. Quick-to-See Smith wants viewers to understand the importance of her Native American heritage. What elements of art has she shown to communicate her idea in the artwork on the opposite page?

Look for another artwork by this artist later in the unit. It also reflects her heritage.

Photography

Some artists express their feelings and ideas through photography. **Photography** is the art and science of making a picture with a **camera.** The pictures on these two pages are **still photographs.** They do not move. They were created by two well-known photographers before color film was invented.

Alfred Stieglitz. *The Steerage,* 1907. Photogravure, 7¹¹⁄₁₆ by 6³⁄₁₆ inches. George Eastman House, Rochester, NY.

Dorothea Lange. *Pledge of Allegiance at Raphael Weill Elementary School a Few Weeks Prior to the Evacuation, San Francisco,* 1942. Black-and-white photograph. © The Dorothea Lange Collection, Oakland Museum of California, City of Oakland. Gift of Paul S. Taylor.

Photographs like these show events that happened in the history of the United States. Both artists framed their photographs carefully. For example, notice the diagonal lines in *The Steerage.* Diagonals frame three sides of the photograph. A fourth diagonal, the ramp, cuts through the middle. These diagonal lines give the photograph a feeling of movement and energy.

How does Lange use unity and variety in her photograph on this page?

Sketchbook Journal

Draw a picture of a camera you might invent. Then write a plan for a photograph you would like to take with your camera. Include details about time of day or lighting and the specific position of your subject.

Studio 1
Make a Photogram

You do not need a camera to take a picture. You can make a photogram. Photograms are pictures made of light and shadow on special paper. Follow these steps.

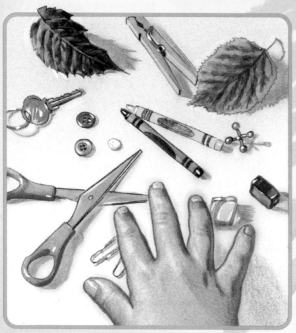

1 Gather a variety of small objects with interesting shapes.

2 Fold newsprint in half. Inside this folder, place a sheet of blueprint paper.

Technique Tip

Collect solid objects as well as objects you can see through. The light affects each object differently.

3 Arrange objects on the blueprint paper. Close the folder. Go outside and open it.

4 When the paper turns white, close the folder. Back inside, dip the paper in water.

Think Like an Artist

How did you use the elements of art and principles of design to unify your photogram?

Photomontage Art

Photographers are not limited to using only one image in an artwork. After printing a photograph, artists can cut it apart and add it to other pieces of photographs to create a **photomontage.**

Ludwig Mies van der Rohe. *Concert Hall,* 1942. Collage over photograph, 29½ by 62 inches. The Mies van der Rohe Archive, The Museum of Modern Art, New York.

David Hockney. *Brooklyn Bridge, Nov. 28, 1982,* 1982. Photographic collage, 109 by 58 inches. Edition: 20. Brooklyn Museum of Art, Brooklyn, NY. © David Hockney.

Composition is the way the parts of an artwork are arranged. German architect Ludwig Mies van der Rohe created the artwork on page 192 by arranging shapes and images on top of a photograph of a building. Because he used more than one medium, his work is referred to as **mixed media.**

British artist David Hockney created a different kind of composition. He used parts of different photographs, but each photograph was a picture of the same thing. What feeling do you get from his composition?

Sketchbook Journal

Cut part of a photograph out of a magazine. Glue it into your Sketchbook Journal. Create a composition by drawing over and around it. Write a description of your artwork.

Studio 2

Create a Photomontage

A photomontage is a type of collage. Follow the steps to make your own photomontage.

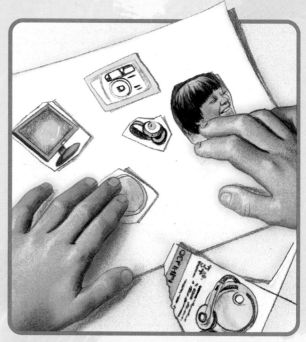

1 Choose a theme or topic. Find and cut out photographs from old magazines.

2 Arrange the photographs to express an idea or a feeling.

Technique Tip

When you are ready to glue your photographs, use a glue stick instead of liquid glue. Liquid glue can cause thin magazine paper to wrinkle.

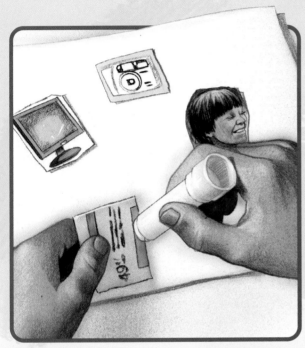

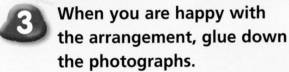 **3** When you are happy with the arrangement, glue down the photographs.

4 Add details with markers, oil pastels, or crayons.

Think Like an Artist

How does your composition, or arrangement, help a viewer understand the meaning of your photomontage?

Moving Pictures

A movie is made up of a series of still photographs. Each picture, or frame, shows the characters or scenery in a slightly different position. As the film runs through a projector, the actors appear to move. A **motion picture,** or movie, is made up of thousands of frames.

Frames from the motion picture *Jurassic Park*

A storyboard artist may make hundreds of drawings while planning an animated film.

Artists can make drawings move too. **Animation** is the art of putting drawings in a sequence and recording them on film. When the film runs through a projector, the drawings seem to be moving, just as in real life. Artists use a **storyboard,** like the one above, to show where the images go.

Some artists record images on videotape instead of film. They may even combine images using video equipment with still photographs, music, or other media. All of these are types of **video art.**

Art Fact

Twenty-four frames of film make up one second of a motion picture. What seems to be a continuous flow of motion is actually separate pictures being flashed onto a screen.

Studio 3

Make a Storyboard

A storyboard is an outline map of a motion picture. It shows the major action and the sounds, or audio. Make a storyboard for a scene, a small segment of a movie.

1 Brainstorm ideas for a movie scene. Choose one whose action you can show clearly.

2 Divide a sheet of paper into three columns. Label them *Notes*, *Video*, and *Audio*.

Technique Tip

Use index cards to work out ideas for your scene. Put one image on each card. Then arrange the cards in an order that makes the action clear.

198

3 Draw each main action. Write instructions to the photographer under *Notes.*

4 Write the characters' words in the *Audio* column. Include any special sounds too.

Think Like an Artist

Does your storyboard contain complete information? Would a photographer and a sound engineer be able to work from your storyboard? Why or why not?

Views of Our Country

Artists use symbols, images that have extra meaning, to make their artwork richer. What symbols of the United States did these two artists use? What do you think each artist is saying about this country?

Jaune Quick-to-See Smith. *Where Do We Come From, What Are We, Where Are We Going,* 2000. Oil and mixed media on canvas, 36 by 48 inches. © Jaune Quick-to-See Smith.

Malcah Zeldis. *Miss Liberty Celebration,* 1987. Oil on corrugated cardboard, 54½ by 36½ inches. Smithsonian American Art Museum, Washington, D.C.

Both artworks express opinions about the United States. But they do it in different ways. How are their styles different? How are they similar?

Notice how Quick-to-See Smith's artwork combines pictures with words. How do these parts support each other? Suppose she had included only the pictures. How would the meaning of her artwork have changed?

How did Zeldis show emphasis? Tell about all the symbols in this composition.

Sketchbook Journal

Write five adjectives, or descriptive words, that describe the country where you were born. Then write the title of an artwork you could make based on those adjectives. Make a sketch showing your ideas.

Surrealism

Surrealism, a dreamlike style of art, is an art movement that developed in the 1920s. Artists who joined this movement showed fantasy images in their artworks that cause viewers to look again. Surrealist artworks combine realistic images with dreamlike ideas.

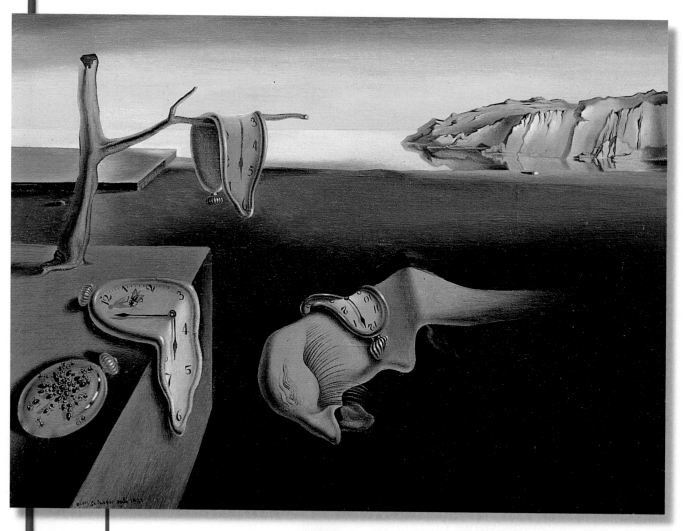

Salvador Dalí. *The Persistence of Memory (Persistance de la mémoire),* 1931. Oil on canvas, 9½ by 13 inches. The Museum of Modern Art, New York. Given anonymously. © 1997 Demart Pro Arte (R), Geneva/Artists Rights Society (ARS), New York. Photogaph © 1996 The Museum of Modern Art, New York.

René Magritte. *Golconde,* 1953. Oil on canvas, 31½ by 39 inches. The Menil Collection, Houston, TX.

Surrealists were interested in dreams. To make their paintings appear as dreams, Surrealists combined objects in unexpected ways. What is unexpected about the images in *The Persistence of Memory?*

Look at the painting on this page. The artist created an **illusion,** an image that is not possibly a part of real life. What part of this painting is not possible? How would you describe the mood of each of these paintings?

Sketchbook Journal

Draw a picture in the Surrealist style showing you and your friends moving around as if gravity did not exist. Then write a paragraph describing the way you feel outside the force of gravity.

Paint a Dream Scene

Become a Surrealist. Follow the steps to create a dream scene.

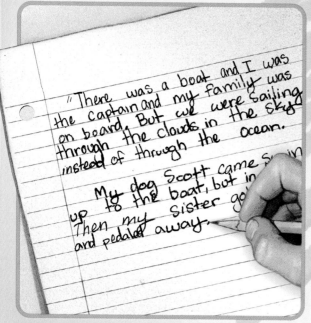

1 Write a summary of a dream you remember. Include all the details you can recall.

2 Draw your dream scene. Include as many details from your dream as you can.

Technique Tip

If you cannot recall your dreams, try this: Keep your Sketchbook Journal by your bed. When you wake up, write down what you recall.

3 Add color to your Surreal composition with tempera paint.

4 Make a frame of colored construction paper.

Think Like an Artist

What dreamlike elements did you include? What elements appear to be real?

Pop Art and Op Art

Can you imagine using a picture from a soup can as the subject for an artwork? That is the sort of artwork that some American artists created during the 1960s. They borrowed ideas from advertisements and even comic strips to create **Pop Art,** which is short for "popular art." Anything that was popular was fair game for Pop Artists.

Roy Lichtenstein. *Still Life with Crystal Bowl,* 1973. Oil and synthetic polymer on canvas, 52 by 42 inches. Collection of Whitney Museum of American Art, Purchased with funds from Frances and Sydney Lewis. Photograph by Geoffrey Clements. © 1995 Whitney Museum of American Art, New York.

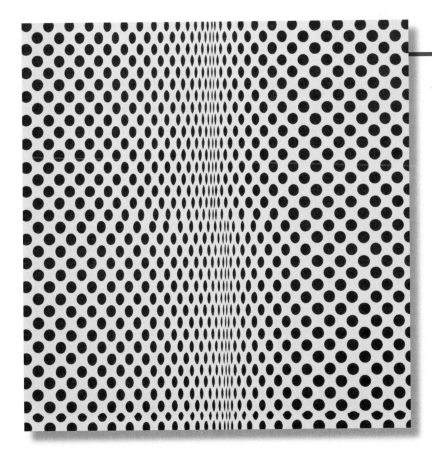

Bridget Riley. *Fission,* 1963. Tempera on composition board, 35 by 34 inches. Museum of Modern Art, New York.

The bend in the surface is an optical illusion.

The still life on page 206 is an example of Pop Art. It reflects the bright, flat colors of comic strips. The forms are simplified. The artist showed depth with overlapping. Lines and shading give the bowl depth, but the fruit shapes are flat and without shading.

The painting on this page is an example of optical art, or **Op Art.** Can you guess why? Op Artists, also practicing during the 1960s, created optical illusions. They could fool the eye simply by repeating lines or shapes in various sizes and positions.

Sketchbook Journal

Draw lines and shapes that play tricks on your eye. How did you create optical illusions in your drawing? Describe a technique you used. Write about any problems you had.

Draw a Pop Art Sound

What does a sound look like? Follow the steps to portray a sound in a Pop Art style.

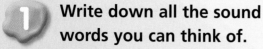

1 Write down all the sound words you can think of.

2 Choose one of the sound words. Draw ideas for how you could show that sound.

Technique Tip

Clean your paintbrush thoroughly between colors. Even a little speck of color on your brush could muddy your next color.

3 Transfer your best sketch to a sheet of paper. Add a border like a cartoon frame.

4 Paint your drawing in bright, Pop Art colors.

Think Like an Artist

Describe the colors and shapes you used. How do they convey your sound? Tell how your artwork reflects the Pop Art style.

Jewelry, Old and New

For centuries, people have used bones, shells, metal, and pretty stones to make **jewelry** to wear. In some cultures, jewelry is valued because it is a symbol of power. What kinds of jewelry do you associate with power? Most jewelry is meant to decorate the wearer. What kinds of jewelry do you like?

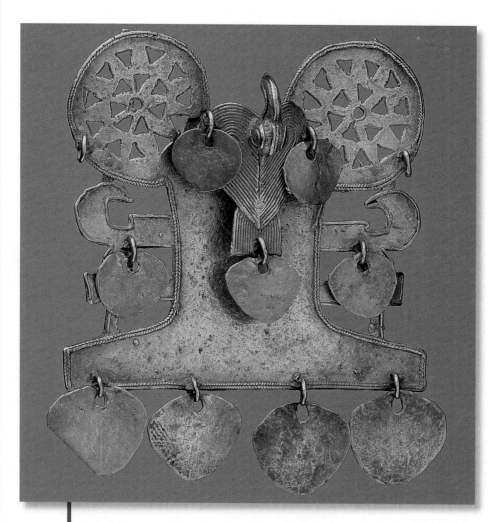

Artist unknown, Colombia, Muisca culture. *Pendant with Bird,* 10th–16th century. Cast gold, height 4½ inches. The Metropolitan Museum of Art, The Michael C. Rockefeller Memorial Collection, bequest of Nelson A. Rockefeller, 1979 (1979.206.526). Photograph © 2001 The Metropolitan Museum of Art, New York.

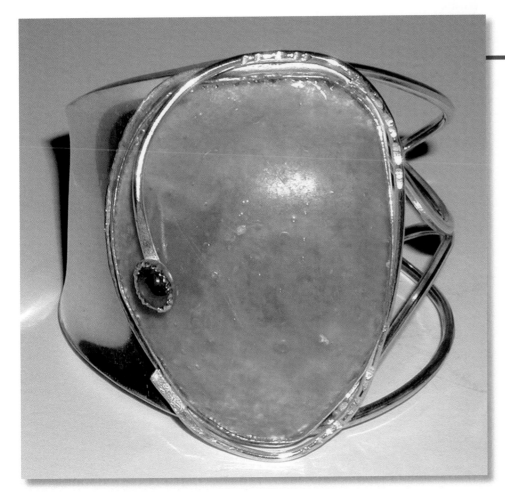

Look at the jewelry on page 210. It is a **pendant,** an object that hangs from a chain or string. It was made more than five hundred years ago by an artist in South America. Notice how the designs on the right side are the same as the designs on the left side. What kind of balance does the pendant show?

The photograph on this page shows a **bracelet,** or jewelry that was designed to be worn on the wrist. This bracelet is modern. What kind of balance did the artist choose for this bracelet?

Sketchbook Journal

Draw a picture of yourself wearing an original work of jewelry art. Show emphasis by including only the part of yourself that shows the jewelry. Then write a short poem about how you feel wearing it.

Design a Bracelet

Express yourself with jewelry. Follow the steps to make a bracelet out of wire and other objects.

1 Make a sketch of some ideas for your bracelet.

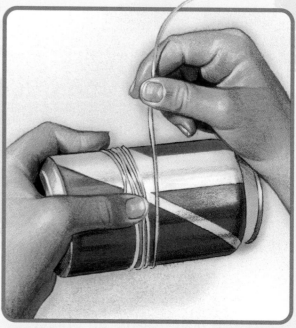

2 Wrap telephone wire around a soda can three or four times.

Technique Tip

Bend the ends of the wire so they will not cut into your skin when you wear your bracelet.

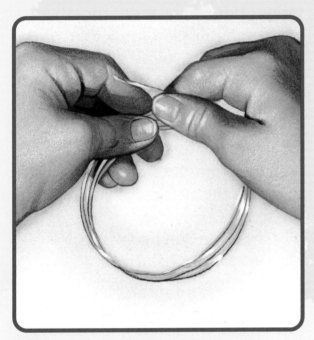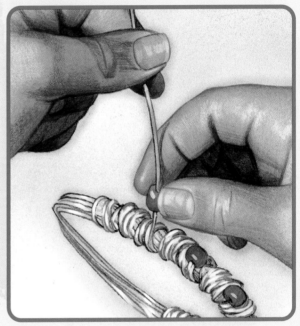

3 Slip the wire off the can. Wrap the ends around to secure them.

4 Tightly wrap metallic wire around the telephone wire. Slide beads on as you wrap.

Think Like an Artist

How did you show principles of design in your bracelet? Which principles stand out most?

Storyboard Art

Catherine Yuh Rader has created storyboards for some popular animated films.

Catherine Yuh Rader is a storyboard artist. Storyboards are sketches that show what each shot of an animated movie will be. Filmmakers use storyboards as "maps" for filming.

Artists like Rader work from the written script to plan what each scene will look like. Details include where the scene takes place and what the characters are saying. Artists also show how the characters act and look, and from what angle the audience views the scene. The series of drawings is put together in a computer slide show that includes music, voices, and sound effects. The director uses this rough sketch version of each scene to get an overview of the finished movie. Animators then use the sketches from the storyboard artist to create the characters you see on the screen.

Catherine Yuh Rader says, "There are tons of career opportunities for people who enjoy drawing and painting. When I was a kid, my sisters and I always sat around and drew because it was fun. I can't believe that now that I'm grown, I get paid for drawing pictures all day."

These sketches are examples of storyboard art by Catherine Yuh Rader.

Make Photocopy Art

Many artists use technology as one of their media. Follow the steps to make a high-tech painting with a photocopy machine.

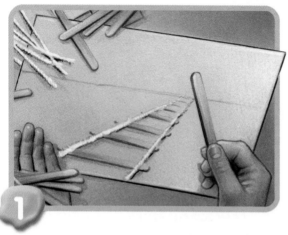

1

Arrange flat objects, such as craft sticks or pipe cleaners, to show a place you like to go.

2

Glue down the arrangement you like best. Let it dry.

3

Photocopy your design. Add color to the photocopy with markers or paint.

4

Finish coloring your picture. You may add optical illusions.

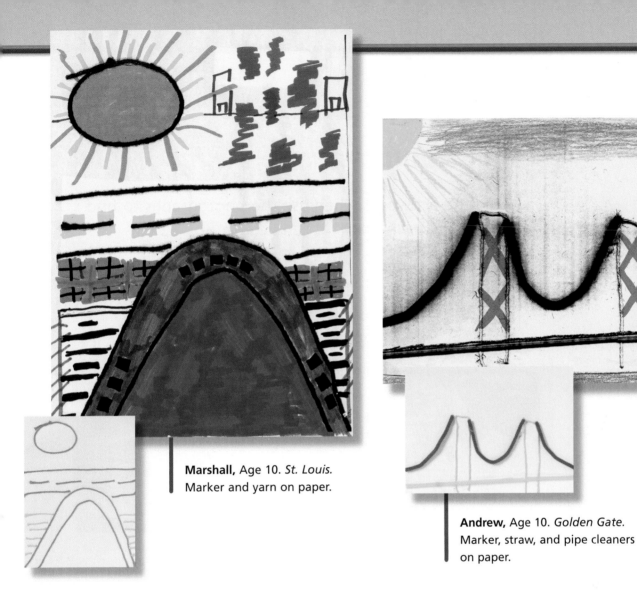

Marshall, Age 10. *St. Louis.*
Marker and yarn on paper.

Andrew, Age 10. *Golden Gate.*
Marker, straw, and pipe cleaners
on paper.

How did these students turn
photocopies into artworks?

Share Your Art

1. Describe the place you chose to show in your artwork.

2. Describe the hardest part of the project. Explain how
you overcame its challenges.

3. If you created an Op Art illusion, explain how.

Think About Art

Read the art words. Then use the photographs to find an example of each word.

still photograph   bracelet   jewelry
Surrealism   camera

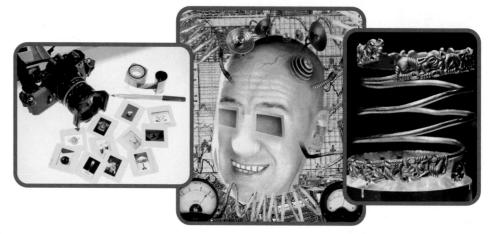

Write About Art

Plan a photomontage portrait of your best friend. Write about the feelings you want to express in your artwork. Describe the types of photographs you will use. Explain how you will express your ideas.

Talk About Art

- Look through your Sketchbook Journal and portfolio.
- Choose the artwork that was the most fun to create.
- Tell a friend why you enjoyed making it.
- Describe the artwork's style and the medium or media you used.

Manuel Alvarez Bravo.
The Daydream, 1931.
Gelatin silver print, 8 by
10 inches. Fred Jones Jr.
Museum of Art, The
University of Oklahoma,
Norman, OK. Gift of
Dr. and Mrs. Richard L.
Sandor, 2000.

Put It All Together

1. What is the girl in this photograph doing? Where is she?

2. How do the diagonal and vertical lines of the railing affect the composition?

3. What mood does the photographer capture?

4. Do you think the photographer captured the girl in this pose without her knowing? Or did he pose the girl in this position? Explain your answer.

Line

straight

curved

zigzag

thin

thick

broken

Color

cool

warm

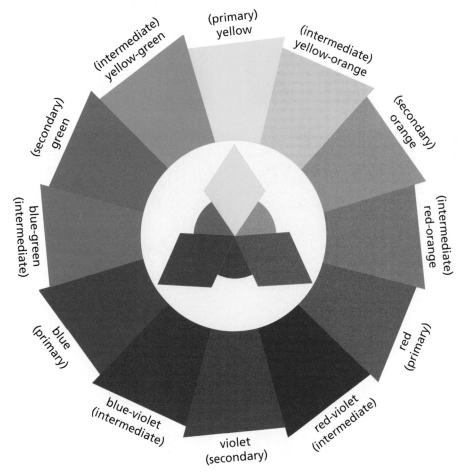

color wheel

Value

Shape

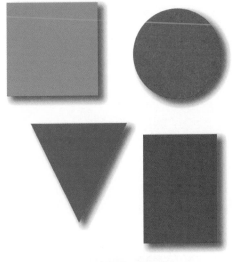

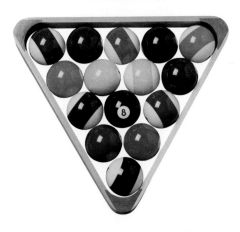

geometric shapes | **organic shapes**

Texture

bumpy

soft

shiny

prickly

sticky

fluffy

Form

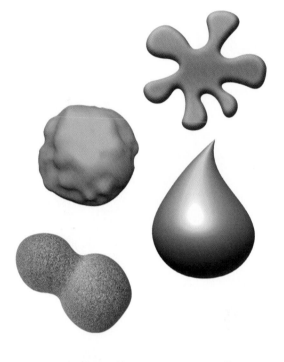

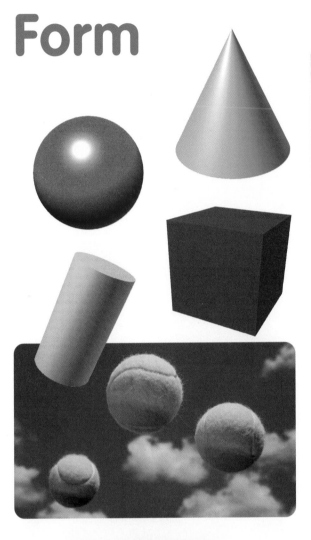

geometric forms

organic forms

Space

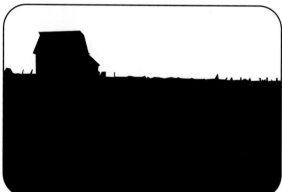

positive space

negative space

Unity

Variety

Emphasis

Balance

Proportion

Pattern

Rhythm

Think Safety

Read these safety rules. Be sure to follow these rules when you create artworks.

1. Keep art materials away from your face, especially your mouth and eyes.

2. Be careful when you work with scissors. If you use a sharp object, point it away from your body.

3. Read the labels on art materials. Look for the word *nontoxic*. This label tells you the materials are safe to use.

4. Do not breathe chalk dust or art sprays.

5. If you have a problem with any art materials, ask your teacher for help.

6. If an art material makes you feel sick, tell your teacher right away.

7. If you spill water or paint on the floor, be sure to clean it up quickly. A wet floor is unsafe to walk on.

8. Clean up after you finish an artwork. First, wash your hands with soap and water. Then, wash the tools you want to save, such as paintbrushes. Return art materials to their proper places.

Can you think of more ways to be safe?

List of Artists

Unknown Artists

Artists

List of Artists

Glossary

A

abstract [ab strakt´] A style of art in which the subject of an artwork has been simplified or rearranged. Abstract art emphasizes moods and impressions and is characterized by the use of bold colors, lines, and flat shapes.

Abstract Expressionism [ab strakt´ ik spre´ shə ni zəm] A nonrepresentational style of art in which the artist often showed the main feeling or action of the subject rather than every detail by pouring or spattering paint onto the canvas. Abstract Expressionism became a dominant style of art after World War II and remained so through the 1960s.

actual line A line that is real. It is a line you can actually see.

additive method [a´ də tiv me´ thəd] A method of creating a sculpture by combining, attaching, or adding separate parts to create a whole. Assemblages and welded metal sculptures are examples of artworks created through this method.

analogous [ə na´ lə gəs] **color scheme** A color scheme made up of colors that are next to each other on the color wheel (for example, yellow, yellow-orange, and orange). They are also called *related colors*.

animation The process of showing in rapid succession a series of drawings or photographs, each image having a small change in the position of the subject(s). This process creates the illusion of motion.

architecture [är´ kə tek chər] The art and science of designing buildings and other large-scale, functional structures.

armature [är´ mə chùr] In sculpture, a framework used to support material, such as clay or papier-mâché, that is being formed.

art history The study of the historical and cultural contexts of artworks and artists.

art movement A recognized style in art history created by a group of artists often working in the same time and place, whose techniques are similar.

art museum A building where collections of artworks and other objects are exhibited and cared for.

assemblage [ə sem´ blij] A type of three-dimensional art created by combining and connecting a variety of objects to create a unified whole.

asymmetrical [ā sə me´ tri kəl] **balance** A type of balance in which two sides of an artwork are not alike but carry equal or nearly equal visual weight. It is also known as *informal balance*.

asymmetry [ā si´ mə trē] A type of balance that lacks symmetry.

audio The part of video or television equipment or storyboarding that deals with sound.

background The part of an artwork that appears to be farthest from the viewer, often in the distance of a scene.

balance The arrangement of the parts of an artwork to give an overall sense of equality in visual weight. Balance can be symmetrical, asymmetrical, or radial. Balance is a principle of design.

brayer [brā´ ər] In printing, a rubber roller used to spread ink over a surface.

C

camera An art tool or instrument used to take photographs.

center of interest The part of an artwork the viewer notices first. It is the most important part of an artwork.

ceramic [sə ra´ mik] A hard material made by baking, or firing, clay. It is also the artwork made of the ceramic.

clay A powdery substance found in the earth that becomes pliable, or flexible, when moistened and hardens when baked. Clay is used to create artworks such as sculpture and pottery.

coil method A technique of creating clay forms using long, round pieces of clay called coils. The coils are wound like a spiral, one atop the other.

collage [kə läzh´] An artwork created by arranging and gluing small pictures or photographs, pieces of paper, fabric, or other materials, onto a larger, flat surface.

color The visual quality of objects, as they reflect hues on the color wheel, caused by the amount of light reflected by them. Color is an element of art.

color scheme A plan for combining color in an artwork.

commercial art Art that has been produced for advertising and other profit-making industries.

Artist unkown. *Feria de Seville*, 1965.

239

complementary color scheme
A color scheme that uses colors that contrast strongly with one another. Complementary colors are directly opposite one another on the color wheel.

composition [käm pə zi´ shən]
The arrangement of the various parts of an artwork into a pleasing whole. Composition also refers to a work of art.

constructed environment An environment containing objects or features that have been planned and built by people.

contemporary style A current, modern way of creating art through the use of various media, methods, materials, and subjects. See *style*.

contrast To show a large difference between two elements of art.

cool colors Related colors that range from green through blue and violet. Cool colors bring to mind cool objects, places, and feelings.

craftsperson An artist who creates a craft such as furniture, pottery, and quilts.

design A plan for arranging the elements of an artwork. Also the creative and organized arrangement of elements of an artwork.

detail A small part of an artwork that has been pulled out and usually enlarged for close inspection. A detail is also a tiny or particularly interesting part of an artwork.

diagonal line A line that slants in one direction. A diagonal line is neither vertical nor horizontal.

elements of art The basic parts of an artwork, including line, color, value, shape, texture, form, and space.

emphasis [em´ fə səs] The visual accent, stress, or sense of importance created in an artwork by the color, size, shape, or placement of an object or area. Emphasis is a principle of design.

Expressionistic
[ik spre shə nis´ tik] A style of art in which the artist boldly expresses personal experiences and emotions about a subject using simple designs and brillant colors. Expressionism began in Germany during the 1900s.

It became popular in the United States during the 1940s and 1950s.

Eye-Dazzler Blanket A blanket woven in a specific and traditional Navajo style, with intricate patterns of bright colors.

fire To bake clay in a kiln. Firing causes the clay to retain its hardness.

foreground The part of an artwork that appears to be nearest the viewer.

form A three-dimensional object, such as a cube or a sphere, that is shown in three-dimensional artworks. Form is defined by height, depth, and width. Form is an element of art.

frontal view In an artwork, a view of the front side of an object or person.

functional art Art created and used for a specific purpose.

geometric shape A shape that is mathematically defined or regular in appearance, such as a triangle, circle, square, or rectangle.

German Expressionism
[ik spre′ shə niz əm] A style of art developed in Germany in the early 1900s. The German Expressionists used bright, bold colors and expressed feelings in their artworks.

glaze A glassy substance that is applied to clay before firing in a kiln. It forms a hard surface that can protect the clay and serve as decoration.

graphic design The design and often the production of commercial artworks, such as signs, posters, advertisements, book jackets, and computer software.

guidelines Lines marked on drawing paper to use as a guide in placing the facial features for a portrait.

horizon line The line created in an artwork by the meeting of sky and ground, usually on the viewer's eye level.

horizontal line The direction of a line running straight across, parallel to the horizon.

illusion [i lü´zhən] An image that tricks the eye or seems to be something it is not.

illustration A picture, often a drawing or painting, created mostly to be shown in books, magazines, or other printed works. An illustration helps explain something, or tells a story.

illustrator An artist who creates pictures for books, magazines, or other printed works to help clarify the text.

implied line A line that is not shown but is implied, or suggested, by the placement of other lines, shapes, and colors.

industrial design The design of objects, such as automobiles, appliances, and telephones, manufactured and sold by industry.

intermediate color A color created when a primary color (yellow, red, or blue) is mixed with a secondary color (orange, violet, or green). Some examples are red-violet and blue-green.

jewelry Ornaments or decorative objects that people wear, such as rings, bracelets, and necklaces. Artists design and make jewelry.

kiln A hot oven used to bake and harden artworks made of clay, such as pottery or ceramics.

L

landscape An artwork showing an outdoor scene or scenery.

landscape architecture The art of planning and designing outdoor areas such as gardens and parks.

line The thin path of a point usually created by a pen, pencil, or paintbrush. Lines can be actual or implied. Line is an element of art. A line can be thick or thin and can be curved, straight, zigzag, wavy, spiral, or broken. Line is an element of art.

loom [lüm´] A frame-like tool used to hold fibers for weaving fabric.

M

media The materials used to create artworks, such as charcoal, pastels, oil paints, or clay. Media also refers to the techniques used to make an artwork, such as painting, sculpting, or drawing. The singular of *media* is *medium*.

middle ground The part of an artwork that appears to lie between the foreground and the background.

mixed media Artworks created by using more than one medium. For example, collage can be a mixed-media artwork in which drawing, painting, and photography are combined.

model Someone or something the artist uses as an example when creating an artwork. Also, in architecture, a model is a small version that represents a larger building or structure.

monochromatic [mä nə krō mā´ tik] **color scheme** A color scheme that consists of tints and shades of only one hue.

mosaic [mō zā´ ik] An artwork created by setting tesserae into mortar or onto another adhesive background to create a unified pattern or image. See *tesserae*.

Artist unknown, Roman. *Mosaic-Two Roman Figures.*

motif [mō tēf´] An element that is repeated often enough to be an important feature of a design.

motion Movement; a change in posture or position. In art, the depiction of movement or change.

motion picture A series of slightly changing images recorded on a filmstrip. When viewed in rapid succession, the rapidly changing images create the illusion of continuous motion.

movement In an artwork, a quality that evokes a sense of action, often created using lines or patterns.

mural [myŭr´ əl] A large artwork, usually a painting, applied to a wall or ceiling. Murals often appear on or in public buildings.

natural environment A natural setting that has not been changed by humans.

negative space The empty space that surrounds a form or shape in an artwork.

neutrals A term used for black, white, and tints and shades of gray. Some artists also consider brown to be neutral.

nonobjective [nän əb jek´ tiv] **style** A term used to describe artworks that have no recognizable subject matter. This style does not represent real objects.

object Something in an artwork that usually can be named by the viewer.

Op Art A style of art in which artists create the illusion of movement or other optical illusions. Op Art, short for Optical Art, was developed in the 1950s and 1960s.

organic shape Shapes and forms that are irregular, particularly those resembling objects in nature, such as the shape of a leaf or the form of an animal.

overlapping Partly or completely covering one shape or form with another.

pattern Repetition of color, line, shape, or form in an artwork. Pattern is a principle of design. Also, a pattern is a plan or model to be followed when making something.

pendant An ornament attached to a necklace or other piece of jewelry.

perspective Techniques for showing three-dimensional objects or scenes on a flat surface.

photograph An image recorded by a camera on film. The image can be printed on photosensitive paper, or if the camera is digital, the image can be shown on a computer screen.

photography The art of creating photographs.

photomontage [fō tō män täzh´] An artwork made by combining parts of different photographs.

plate See *printing block*.

Pop Art A style of art developed during the 1950s. Pop Artists show people, objects, or scenes from popular culture and use graphics similar to those found in advertisements or comic strips.

portrait [pōr´ trət] An artwork that features a person, an animal, or a group of people, often placing emphasis on the face.

positive space Shapes, forms, or lines that stand out from the background or negative space in an artwork.

poster A large printed sign or notice, often illustrated with artwork and other images. It is often placed on a wall or another large surface to announce an event or to convey other information.

primary color One of the three colors (yellow, red, and blue) from which other colors are made.

principles of design Guidelines artists use to arrange elements of art. The principles of design are unity, variety, emphasis, balance, proportion, pattern, and rhythm.

print An artwork created by coating a surface, such as a carved wood block, with wet color and then pressing paper onto it. The paper is "pulled" as a print.

printing block A surface, such as wood or linoleum, into which an artist carves a design. Ink or paint is spread across the surface and paper is pressed onto it to make a print, an impression of the design. A block is also known as a *plate*.

profile Something that is seen or shown from the side, such as a side view of a face.

proportion [prə pōr´ shən] The size relationship of one part of an artwork to another part or to the whole. For example, the size relationship of the nose to the face shows proportion. Proportion is a principle of design.

R

radial [rā´ dē əl] **balance** A type of balance in which lines or shapes spread out from a center point.

realistic A style of art that describes artworks showing objects and scenes as they actually look to most viewers.

relief [ri lēf´] **print** An artwork made by rolling ink onto a carved surface showing a raised design and then pressing paper onto it.

relief sculpture [ri lēf´ skəlp´ chər] A kind of sculpture that stands out from a flat background.

repertoire [re´ pə twär] The skills and knowledge of a person or group.

rhythm [ri´ thəm] A sense of visual movement or motion caused by the repetition of one or more elements of art, such as color, line, shape, or form, in an artwork. Rhythm is a principle of design.

scene In a motion picture, a series of shots showing events that occur in one place over a short period of time.

score To scratch, mark, or cut a wet clay surface with a tool prior to joining the clay parts.

sculpture [skəlp´ chər] An artwork made by modeling, carving, or joining materials into a three-dimensional whole. Clay, wood, stone, and metal are some common materials used for sculpture. Sculpture is also the process of making such an artwork.

secondary color A color created by mixing two primary colors. The secondary colors are orange (made from yellow and red), violet (made from red and blue), and green (made from blue and yellow).

self-portrait [self´ pōr´ trət] An artwork showing a likeness of the artist who created it.

shade A darker value created by adding black to a color or by adding black to white.

shading techniques Techniques by which an artist shows gradual changes in darker values of an artwork. Shading helps make an artwork appear more three-dimensional.

shape A two-dimensional flat area made by lines that enclose it. A shape can be geometric, such as a circle or square, or organic, having an irregular outline. Shape is an element of art.

silversmith An artist who creates objects from silver.

slab method A method of creating pottery by joining flat forms cut from slabs of clay.

slip Clay that has been thinned with water to a creamy consistency. Slip is used to join scored pieces of clay and to decorate pottery.

space An open or empty surface or area. Shapes and forms show empty space surrounding them (negative space) and the space they occupy (positive space). Space is an element of art.

still life An artwork showing an arrangement of objects that do not move on their own.

still photograph A photograph that does not move, as compared to a motion picture.

storyboard A series of drawings that represent the visual and audio plan of a video production.

style An artist's own special way of creating art through the use of specific media, methods, materials, or subjects. Artistic style can also represent certain techniques of a group of artists in a specific culture or time.

subject What an artwork is about. It can be a person, object, or scene. A subject is the recognizable topic of an artwork.

subtractive method [səb trak´ tiv me´ thəd] A method of creating a sculpture by carving, cutting, or otherwise removing excess material from a block of wood, stone, clay, or other substance.

Surrealism [sə rē´ə li zəm] A movement in art from the early twentieth century that expresses strange dreams, subconscious thoughts, and often fantastic and unreal images.

Salvador Dali. *The Persistence of Memory,* 1931.

symbol [sim´ bəl] A letter, color, sign, or picture used to represent a word, message, or idea. For example, a red heart is often used as a symbol for love.

symmetrical [sə me´ tri kəl] **balance** A type of balance in which both sides of a center line are the same or about the same. A cat's face, for example, is symmetrically balanced along a vertical line through the middle of the nose. Symmetrical balance is also known as *formal balance.*

symmetry [si´ mə trē] Balance created by making both sides of an artwork the same or about the same.

tactile texture [tak´ təl teks´ chər] Texture that can be understood by the sense of touch. It is also called *actual texture.* Tactile textures, which artists show in their compositions, include rough, smooth, silky, pebbly, soft, hard, bumpy, and scratchy. See *texture.*

tesserae [te´ sə rə] In a mosaic, the small pieces of glass, tile, stones, paper, or similar material set into mortar or onto another adhesive surface to create a unified pattern.

texture [teks´ chər] The way a surface feels (actual or tactile texture) or looks (visual texture). Words such as shiny, dull, rough, and smooth are used to describe texture. Texture is an element of art.

three-dimensional Having height, width, and depth or thickness. Something that is three-dimensional is not a flat shape. It is a form.

tint A light value of a color created by mixing the color with white.

traditional style A style that conforms to knowledge, beliefs, and customs passed down from one generation to the next.

two-dimensional Having height and width but not depth. Something that is two-dimensional is flat.

unity [yü´ nə tē] A quality that occurs when all parts of an artwork combine to create a sense of wholeness and completion. Unity is a principle of design.

value [val´ yü] The lightness or darkness of a color. Tints have a light value. Shades have a dark value. For example, pink is a light value of red, while navy is a dark value of blue. Value is an element of art.

vanishing point In an artwork using linear perspective, the point at which converging lines meet.

variety The combination of elements of art, such as line, shape, or color, that adds extra interest to an artwork. Variety is a principle of design.

vertical line A line that goes straight up and down.

visual texture [vi´ zhə wəl teks´ chər] The way a surface appears through the sense of vision. For example, the surface of a sculpture may be shiny or dull. See *texture*.

warm colors The family of related colors that range from yellow through orange and red. Warm colors usually remind people of warm objects, places, and feelings.

warp [wȯrp´] In weaving, fibers stretched vertically, top to bottom, on a loom and through which the weft is woven.

weaving An artwork made of woven thread, yarn, or other fibers or materials.

weft In weaving, fibers woven from side to side, over and under, through the warp on a loom.

Artist unknown, Navajo culture.
Navajo Pictorial Blanket, ca. 1890.

248

Index

Index

Acknowledgments

ILLUSTRATIONS

20, 21, 24, 25, 28, 29, 34, 35, 38, 39, 42, 43, 54, 55, 58, 59, 62, 63, 68, 69, 72, 73, 76, 77, 88, 89, 92, 93, 96, 97, 102, 103, 106, 107, 110, 111, 122, 123, 126, 127, 130, 131, 136, 137, 140, 141, 144, 145, 156, 157, 160, 161, 164, 165, 170, 171, 174, 175, 178, 179, 190, 191, 194, 195, 198, 199, 204, 205, 208, 209, 212, 213 Roger Motzkus

46, 80, 114, 148, 182, 216 Steven Chorney

PHOTOGRAPHS

Every effort has been made to secure permission and provide appropriate credit for photographic material. The publisher deeply regrets any omission and pledges to correct errors called to its attention in subsequent editions.

Unless otherwise acknowledged, all photographs are the property of Scott Foresman, a division of Pearson Education.

Photo locators denoted as follows: Top (t), Center (c), Bottom (b), Left (l), Right (r), Background (Bkgd)

Front Matter

Page 1(br), Grandma Moses: *December.* Copyright © 1952 (renewed 1980)/Grandma Moses Properties Co., New York; 5(br), © Christie's Images /Corbis; 7, © Sheldan Collins/Corbis; 7, Denver Art Museum Collection. Gift of Exeter Drilling Company and Mr. and Mrs. Morris A. Long, 1979.3. © Photo by Denver Art Museum. All rights reserved; 7, Musée d'Art Moderne de la Ville de Paris, France/Giraudon, Paris/SuperStock; 10, Photo by Steve Pitkin/Pitkin Studios, provided by Tinwood Alliance collection, Atlanta, GA; 14, © Fiduciario en el Fideicomiso relativo a los Museos Diego Rivera y Frida Kahlo. Reproduction authorized by the Bank of Mexico, Mexico City.

Units 1–6

Page 16, Art Institute of Chicago, Helen Birch Bartlett Memorial Collection, 1926.224. Photograph © 1996, The Art Institute of Chicago. All rights reserved; 17, Ernest Laurent. *Portrait of Georges Seurat,* 1883. Musée du Louvre, Paris, France. Réunion des Musées Nationaux/Art Resource, NY; 18, © Digital Stock; 18, © Image Source/SuperStock; 19(t), Francesco Venturi/Corbis; 19, © Dennis Marsico/Corbis; 23, © Brian Vikander/Corbis; 26, © Erich Lessing/Art Resource, New York; 30, © Musée d'Orsay, Paris/Lauros-Giraudon, Paris/SuperStock; 32, Brooklyn Museum of Art, Museum Expedition 1903, Museum Collection Fund, 03.325.3489a; 33(tl), Brooklyn Museum of Art, Gift of Anna Ferris. 30.1478.48; 33(tr), © Erich Lessing/Art Resource, NY; 36, Museum of Fine Arts, Boston, Massachusetts, USA/Bequest of Maxim Karolik/Bridgeman Art Library; 37, © Christie's Images/Corbis; 41, Solomon R. Guggenheim Museum, New York, 59.1529; 44(br), © Barbara Blossom Ashmun; 44(bc), © SuperStock; 44(bl), © Corbis; 45, © Barbara Blossom Ashmun; 48, © Getty Images; 48, © Getty Images; 49, Photograph by Earlie Hudnall, Hudnall's Positive Images; 50, Courtesy of Sally Griffiths, Dallas, TX; 52, Digital Image © The Museum of Modern Art/Licensed by Scala/Art Resource, NY. © 2004 Succession H. Matisse, Paris/ Artists Rights Society (ARS), New York; 53, © Burstein Collection/Corbis; 56, Purchase with funds from the Friends of the Whitney Museum of American Art. Photograph by Sandak,Inc./ Whitney Museum of American Art, New York; 57(tl), Giraudon/Art Resource, NY; 60, © Francis G. Mayer/Corbis; 64, African American Museum, Dallas, TX, Billy R. Allen Collection.; 65, Grandma Moses: *December.* Copyright © 1952 (renewed 1980) Grandma Moses Properties Co., New York; 66, The Nelson-Atkins Museum of Art, Kansas City, Missouri. Purchase: acquired through the generosity of an anonymous donor; 67, © Getty Images; 71(t), © Smithsonian American Art Museum, Washington, D.C./Art Resource, New York; 75, © CNAC/MNAM/Dist Réunion des Musées Nationaux/Art Resource, NY. © 2004 Succession H. Matisse, Paris/Artists Rights Society (ARS), New York; 78(tl), 79, Dwyer & O'Grady, Inc.; 82(tl), © 1990 United States Postal Service. Displayed with permission. All rights reserved. Written authorization from the Postal Service is required to use, reproduce, post, transmit, distribute, or publicly display these images; 82, © Digital Stock; 85, Photo by Tracye Saar; 87(tr), © Bill Varie/ Corbis; 87(tr), © Tom Main/Getty Images; 87(tr), © ThinkStock/SuperStock; 87(tr), © Larry Lee/Corbis; 87(tr), © Ellen Schuster/Getty Images; 87(tl), Brad Sheard/SuperStock; 87(tl), Corbis; 87(tl), digitalvisiononline.com; 87, © Getty Images; 87, digitalvisiononline.com; 87, © Den Reader/SuperStock; 87, digitalvisiononline.com; 87, © Ivar Mjell/Getty Images; 87, © Tim Flach/Getty Images; 87, © Joel Katz/Corbis; 90, © Heini Schneebeli/ Bridgeman Art Library; 94, © Smithsonian American Art Museum, Washington, D.C./Art Resource, NY; 95(r), 95(l), Victoria & Albert Museum, London/Art Resource, NY; 100, © Giraudon/Art Resource, NY; 101, © Richard

Acknowledgments

Hutchings/PhotoEdit; 104, © Erich Lessing/Art Resource, NY; 105(tl), John Bigelow Taylor/Eugene and Claire Bigelow Collection, Fenimore Art Museum/Art Resource, NY; 105(cr), Photo by Claire Garoutte, courtesy Chihuly Studio; 108, Photograph by Cal Kowal, courtesy Carl Solway Gallery; 109, © Bob Rowan; Progressive Image/Corbis; 112(bl), © Barry George; 112(c), © Getty Image; 112(cr), © Getty Images; 112(br), © Arthur S. Aubrey/Getty Images; 113, © Barry George; 116(tc) © Dave Bartruff/Corbis; 116, © Bill Ross/Corbis; 116, © Dave Bartruff/Corbis; 116, © Getty Images; 118, © 2003 Andy Warhol Foundation for the Visual Arts/ARS, New York/The Andy Warhol Foundation, Inc./Art Resource, NY; 119, Andy Warhol. *Self-Portrait,* 1967. Synthetic polymer paint and silkscreen on canvas, 72 by 72 inches. The Andy Warhold Foundation, Inc./Art Resource, NY. © 2004 Andy Warhol Foundation for the Visual Arts/ARS, New York; 124, © Erich Lessing/Art Resource, NY; 132, The Andy Warhol Foundation, Inc./Art Resource, NY. © 2004 Andy Warhol Foundation for the Visual Arts/ARS, New York; 133; Photo by: Michel Monteaux/ Girard Foundation Collection/Museum of International Folk Art, Santa Fe, NM; 134, © The Jewish Museum, NY/Art Resource, NY; 135, Worcester Art Museum, Worcester, Massachusetts; 138, Courtesy of the National Automobile Museum (The Harrah Collection), Reno, Nevada; 139 (tl) © Jose Luis Pelaez, Inc./Corbis; 139(cl), © Getty Images; 139(bl) © Getty Images; 139(c), © William Whitehurst/Corbis; 139(bc), © Francisco Cruz/SuperStock; 139(tr), © Getty Images; 139(cr), © SuperStock; 142, Collection of Carmen Lomas Garza, San Francisco, CA. Photo by Rudy Gómez Photo Arts. Program cover image courtesy of the Texas Book Festival, Austin, TX; 146, © Raquel Aguiñara-Martinez/Courtesy Mexican Fine Arts Center, Chicago; 147, Photo by Kathleen Culbert-Aguilar/Courtesy Mexican Fine Arts Center, Chicago; 150, Index Stock Imagery; 151, © 1983 United States Postal Service. Displayed with permission. All rights reserved; 153, Marc Chagall. *Self-Portrait,* 1959-1968. Museo di Andrea del Castagno, Uffizi, Florence, Italy. Nimatallah/Art Resource, NY. © 2004 Artists Rights Society (ARS), New York/ADAGP, Paris; 155, Albright-Knox Art Gallery, Buffalo, New York. Gift of Seymour H. Knox, Jr., 1976; 158, © National Gallery, London; 162, 163, Texas Department of Commerce/Tourism; 167, © 2004 Estate of Romare Bearden/Licensed by VAGA, New York, NY; 168, © Christie's Images/SuperStock; 169, © Réunion des Musées Nationaux/Art Resource, NY; 173, © Richard Cummins/SuperStock; 180, © Nancy McMillen; 181, Photo courtesy of Laurence Parent. Used with permission by Texas Monthly Custom Publishing; 184, © W. Cody/Corbis; 184, © SuperStock; 184(tc), © Lisa Berkshire/Getty Images; 185, © 2004 Wassily Kandinsky/Artists Rights Society (ARS), New York; 187, Photograph courtesy of Steinbaum Krauss Gallery, New York; 188, © Christie's Images /Corbis; 189, © The Dorothea Lange Collection, Oakland Museum of California, City of Oakland. Gift of Paul S. Taylor; 192, © The Museum of Modern Art/Licensed by Scala/Art Resource, NY; 193, © David Hockney; 196, Jurassic Park © 1993 Universal Pictures/Amblin Entertainment, courtesy of the Everett Collection; 197, © Tony Freeman/PhotoEdit; 201, © Smithsonian American Art Museum, Washington, D.C./Art Resource, NY; 202, The Museum of Modern Art, New York. Given anonymously. Photogaph © 1996 The Museum of Modern Art, New York. © 2004 Demart Pro Arte (R), Geneva/Artists Rights Society (ARS), New York; 203, © Phototheque R. Magritte-ADAGP/Art Resource, NY. © 2004 Charly Herscovici, Brussels/Artists Rights Society (ARS), New York; 206, © Roy Lichtenstein. Collection of Whitney Museum of American Art, Purchase with funds from Frances and Sydney Lewis. Photograph by Geoffrey Clements, copyright © 1995 Whitney Museum of American Art, New York. 77.64; 207, Digital image © Museum of Modern Art/License by Scala/Art Resource, NY; 210, The Michael C. Rockefeller Memorial Collection, Bequest of Nelson A. Rockefeller, 1979. (1979.206.526)/Photograph © 2001 The Metropolitan Museum of Art/Metropolitan Museum of Art; 211, Photo by Esther Hadisutjipto; 214(tl), 215(t), 215(c), 215(b), © Catherine Yuh Rader; 218, © Richard Morrell/Corbis; 218, © Archivo Iconografico, S.A./Corbis; 218, © Getty Images; 218(tl), Corbis; 219, Gift of Dr. and Mrs. Richard L. Sandor, 2000/Collection Fred Jones Jr. Museum of Art, the University of Oklahoma, Norman.

Back Matter
Page 220, © Getty Images; 220, © Corbis; 221, © Getty Images; 221, digitalvisiononline.com; 222, © Darrell Gulin/Corbis; 222, © Eric Crichton/Corbis; 223, © Paul Chauncey/Corbis; 223, © Corbis; 223, © Corbis; 223, © Pat Doyle/Corbis; 224, © Robert Yin/Corbis; 224, David Frazier/© Corbis; 224, © Peter Dazeley/Corbis; 224, © Richard Hamilton Smith/Corbis; 224, © Charles Gold/Corbis; 224, © Lance Nelson/Corbis; 225, © The Purcell Team/Corbis; 225, © Lindsey P. Martin/Corbis; 225, © Nik Wheeler/Corbis; 227, © Randy Faris/Corbis; 228, © Bob Krist/Corbis; 229, © Charles & Josette Lenars/Corbis; 230, © Mark Gibson/Corbis; 231, © Tom Bean/Corbis; 232, © Corbis; 233, © Getty Images; 239, © Getty Images; 239, © Corbis; 240, © Explorer, Paris/SuperStock; 240, © Marco Cristofori/SuperStock; 241, © GoodShoot/SuperStock; 241, © Holton Collection/SuperStock; 242, © Corbis; 242 (cr) ©Michael Boys/Corbis; 243, © Claudia Kunin/Corbis; 243, Corbis; 245 (tr) © Roger Allyn Lee/Corbis; 245 (cl) Roger Allyn Lee/Corbis; 247, SuperStock; 247,© SuperStock; 248, © The Lowe Art Museum, The University of Miami/SuperStock.